WINGS No.6

D0308907

'Rhino':
The Immortal Phantom II

Joe Cupido

Windrow & Greene

© 1993 Windrow & Greene Ltd.
Published in Great Britain 1993 by
Windrow & Greene Ltd.
5 Gerrard Street
London W1V 7LJ

All rights reserved. No part of this
publication may be reproduced or
transmitted in any form or by any
means electronic or mechanical,
including photocopy, recording, or
in any information storage and
retrieval system, without the prior
written permission of the publishers.

A CIP catalogue record for this book
is available from the British Library.

ISBN 1-872004-18-0

Published in the USA by
Specialty Press Publishers
 & Wholesalers Inc.
PO Box 338
Stillwater, MN 55082
(612) 430-2210/800-888-9653

(Title page) Full frontal - an anonymous F-4E suckles JP-4 from a KC-135 over the Midwest, the chipped paintwork on canopy framing, bleed air louvres and intake lips suggesting a hard-worked ship. The WSO keeps a watchful eye on the transaction while the pilot stares transfixed at the boom lights built into the tanker's underbelly. Note the distinctive covers for the WSO's rear view mirrors, these external 'check six' aids being fitted only to the F-4E/G.

'Brown Shoe' Phantom IIs

There is nothing that looks or sounds like a Phantom II, and from this angle two of its most prominent features are strikingly visible - the 'upswept' outer wing panels and the radically anhedralled stabilators. The 'cranked' wing (12 degree dihedral on the outer sections) allowed pilots to dogfight in the F-4 with renewed confidence, following the succession of large, unwieldy interceptors that had populated fighter units of both the US Navy and Air Force. Although a big aircraft, the Phantom II could hold its own in a turning fight down to speeds of around 450 knots thanks to its radical flying surfaces, coupled with the gutsy General Electric J79 turbojets buried in its slab-sided fuselage. With navigation beacons glowing in the weak dusk light, a flat gray pair of F-4Ss from reserve-manned VMFA-112 'Cowboys' taxy back to the ranch at Naval Air Station (NAS) Dallas following a cross-country flight from NAF Andrews, Maryland. The F-4s had been despatched to the East Coast to represent Marine Air Group (MAG) 41, and VMFA-112, at the retirement ceremony of the Phantom II from service with fellow reservists VMFA-321 'Hell's Angels'. Held on 13 July 1991, this memorable occasion left the 'Cowboys' as the last tactical squadron equipped with the F-4 in the Sea Service role.

(Left) By definition of their mission tasking, frontline Navy F-4 units were based close to the large naval yards at Norfolk, Virginia, and San Diego, California. The air stations at Oceana and Miramar were separated by thousands of miles, and aircrews tended to stay within the Pacific or Atlantic fleet communities throughout their careers. Occasionally squadrons would participate in a world cruise with their embarked carrier air wing that would terminate on the opposite coast to 'home plate'. A two-day 'cross-country' would then see the unit cross America and pitch up back in familiar skies. One of the favourite routing points during these tiring sorties was Hill Air Force Base (AFB), Utah, where this F-4J (BuNo 157245) from VF-51 'Screaming Eagles' is seen parked up on the transient ramp.

Photographed in April 1976, this aircraft poses something of a problem for US Navy historians because, according to official sources, VF-51 never flew the J-model Phantom II. Seasoned exponents with the Bravo and November model F-4s, the 'Screaming Eagles' transitioned directly from the more austere naval Phantom IIs to Grumman's potent F-14A Tomcat in mid-1978 - quite where this Juliet fits in the picture remains a mystery. The lack of a traditional all-black squadron fin and the unusually ornate 'Screaming Eagles' titling on the spine do little to confirm VF-51's ownership of 157245. This aircraft was eventually upgraded to F-4S specs four years later, and finally retired from active service to the Aircraft Maintenance and Regeneration Center (AMARC) at Davis-Monthan AFB, Arizona, on 29 August 1985; the airframe was allocated the ID number 8F205 prior to being stored. VF-51 had distinguished themselves with the F-4B over Vietnam 14 years earlier whilst on their first war cruise with the type aboard USS *Coral Sea* (CV-43) in 1971/72. During the WestPac the squadron downed four MiG-17s, which added to the two MiG-21s claimed by the 'Screaming Eagles' in 1968 whilst equipped with F-8H Crusaders aboard USS *Bon Homme Richard* (CVA-31). VF-51 flew a total of eight combat cruises between 1969 and 1975.

Photographed in sunny Florida a month earlier than 157245, this colorful F-4J was the property of VF-101 'Grim Reapers' during the Bicentennial year. Never known to set the world alight with garishly decorated aircraft, VF-101 used the celebrations of 1976 as an excuse to paint the slab fins of their F-4s in a suitably patriotic scheme. Just in case the casual observer failed to realise the significance of this marking, the paint shop at NAS Oceana added the titling '1776-1976' in gold lettering on the base of the fin. Like many other F-4Js, 155834 was modified to S-specs and reissued to a frontline unit in the early 1980s, although it failed to end its days at Davis-Monthan. When this photograph was taken in March 1976, VF-101 was nearing the end of its association with the Phantom II, the unit retiring its final F-4J in favour of the F-14 in July of the following year.

Still actively training naval aviators today in the art of flying the Tomcat, VF-101 was originally activated at NAS Cecil Field, Florida, on 1 May 1952. Initially part of Carrier Air Group 10 (CVG-10), the 'Grim Reapers' flew several types of early generation fleet jet fighters like the F2H-2 Banshee, F4D-1 Skyray and F3H Demon during the 1950s, before commencing the replacement carrier group role in June 1960 with the F4H Phantom II. 'First in Phantoms' on the East Coast, VF-101 was charged with training a new breed of pilot and radar intercept officer (RIO) for the Navy. Faced with a daunting task, VF-101 set up shop at NAS Key West, Florida, and commenced training 'Phantom nuggets'. The squadron moved to Oceana in April 1971, although an F-4 det was maintained in the Florida Keys - the satellite flight was designated VF-171 Detachment Key West in August 1977 when the parent unit retired its last Phantom II.

(Above) The seasonal coastal murk that often blows in during summer mornings on the California coast provides a rather dull canvas for F-4J BuNo 1555563 as the jet closes on the runway at NAS Point Mugu. Assigned to the elite Pacific Missile Test Center (PMTC) flight, this pristine Phantom II (along with its flight mates) was responsible for clearing the ordnance issued to fleet fighter squadrons on both coasts. The flight used more than a dozen Phantom IIs of various marks over the 25-year service span of the F-4. Eventually replaced at the California base by Tomcats and Hornets in the mid-1980s, many PMTC Phantom IIs were flown to AMARC for storage - the last pair were retired from Point Mugu in autumn 1991, thus ending the Navy's 'manned' ties with the Phantom II. Part of the 40-strong F-4J-34-MC batch delivered to the US Navy from St Louis at the height of the Vietnam conflict, BuNo 155563 was never upgraded to F-4J specs.

It is one of the small ironies of the Phantom II saga that the drone-converted QF-4s often look in far better condition dressed up as targets than when they were on strength with fleet units; QF-4N BuNo 1501456 certainly proves the point as it basks in the evening light. Liberally daubed with high-viz dayglo orange paint and 'TARGET' stencilling, this weary warrior from a past decade has been fully converted to the role of the 'aggressor'. Its stage is the vast, fully instrumented, Pacific Ocean range, which covers a 35,000 square mile area 125 miles wide by 250 miles long. The Phantom IIs are retrieved by the Naval Air Weapons Center (NAWC) at Point Mugu from the large desert storage center at Davis-Monthan, or occasionally from the NARF at NAS North Island, San Diego. After overhauling the airframe at the Naval Aviation Depot at MCAS Cherry Point in North Carolina, and making sure that it will stand up to aggressive anti-missile manoeuvring out over the range, the technicians at the NAWC fit a system of electromechanical servo controls to the Phantom II's flying surfaces, thus allowing the QF-4 to be flown from the 'shirt sleeves' environment of the Threat Simulation Directorate control center at Point Mugu.

Although one of the latest Phantom IIs converted for drone work, this QF-4N still retains its manned capabilities, hence the civilian crew names on the canopy rail. Used as cross-country hacks, and occasionally as touring targets for simulated missile attack profiles for fighter squadrons based some distance from Point Mugu, the small QF-4N force fulfill a multitude of tasks. Aside from the matt Tactical Paint Scheme (TPS) centerline tank, BuNo 153065 is also equipped with an electronic signals emitter pod on the port Sidewinder pylon - this device will further accentuate the aircraft's radar profile, thus allowing an F-14 RIO to track its progress more effectively prior to a simulated missile shoot.

The first drones converted for the NAWC in the early 1970s were restricted in their ability to perform high-G turns, and had a limited pitch-and-roll rate. However, the 31 (as of December 1992) QF-4Ns modified in a program that commenced in 1984 can simulate any manoeuvre flown by a manned Phantom II. Since the 'second generation' drones entered service at Point Mugu in 1986 thousands of hours have been flown by the QF-4s over the Pacific. Up to the end of 1990 the fleet had performed 26 'Ensign Nolo' ('no live operator') sorties against Tomcat and Hornet crews, and only six QF-4s had been successfully downed by missiles fired.

The CO's jet is always maintained in the best possible condition, the '00' modex assuring that the aircraft receives that little bit of extra attention. Although only two months away from its retirement from Marine Corps service, F-4N BuNo 152981 looks as good as it did the day it departed Lambert Field, Missouri, almost two decades before. Photographed on a typically hot summer's day at Marine Corps Air Station (MCAS) El Toro, California, in July 1982, 'Rattler 00' hails from VMFA-323, and is equipped with a single centerline tank and an inert AIM-9 acquisition round on the twin Sidewinder rails above the small travel-pod. Rarely seen wearing a drab scheme during their 19-year association with the Phantom II, the 'Death Rattlers' liberally adorned their F-4s with the distinctive diamond stripes clearly

visible in this photograph. To further add to the color, the crew appear to be wearing old style international orange overalls. The glossy finish and overall showroom condition of this aircraft were no doubt greatly appreciated by its new owners at NAS Miramar upon its arrival in southern California three months after this photograph was taken.

Assigned to VF-154 'Black Knights', the aircraft was immediately resprayed in ultra matt TPS grays and the mirror-like finish was lost forever. 'Black Knight 102' was despatched to NAS Fallon, Nevada, in October 1982, and participated in extensive air wing work-ups with the other members of CVW-14. The aircraft finally put to sea for the last time on 21 March 1983 when VF-154 flew aboard USS *Coral Sea* (CV-43) for the squadron's final world

cruise with the Phantom II. Serving as XO Cdr. John C. Bates' mount throughout the deployment, the jet finally returned to Norfolk Navy Yard on 12 September, the squadron bidding farewell to the *Coral Sea* and heading back to Miramar. F-4N-28-MC BuNo 152981 eventually made its final flight on 19 October 1983 when it was one of five VF-154 Phantom IIs despatched to AMARC from Miramar.

Returning to its previous owners: the 'Death Rattlers' were initially formed as VMF-323 on 1 August 1943, and equipped with F4U Corsairs. Seeing combat in both World War 2 and Korea with the Chance-Vought fighter, the 'Rattlers' eventually teamed up with the Phantom II in 1963 at Cherry Point, North Carolina. Two bloody combat tours of Vietnam were flown by VMFA-323 during

the mid- to late 1960s, the unit being based at Iwakuni, Japan, in between spells at Chu Lai and Da Nang. Returning to El Toro in March 1969, VMFA-323 soldiered on with the Bravo model Phantom II until it received F-4Ns in 1979. The 'Death Rattlers' created US naval aviation history later that year by undertaking a WestPac cruise aboard the Coral Sea with fellow MAG-11 squadron VMFA-531 'Gray Ghosts'. This is the only time in carrier aviation history that a Navy air wing has been protected by an all-Marine fighter force. The veteran F-4Ns were replaced at El Toro by early production model F/A-18 Hornets in 1983, the transition also coinciding with the toning down of the distinctive 'diamondback snake skin' marking.

In the late 1970s the Corps received the word from 'on high' to tone down the markings worn on their jets, and remove the gloss white undersides that had adorned all their fixed-wing combat aircraft for the past two decades. As is traditionally the case in the US Navy/Marines, each squadron chose to embrace the directive differently, and this hybrid scheme was VMFA-115 'Silver Eagles' interpretation of 'toned down' as worn by their F-4Js at MCAS Beaufort in August 1978. Lacking a suitable shade of gray with which to pick out the traditionally black unit and service titling, VMFA-115's paint shop decided on white, and in the process created a distinctive deviation from the standard combat aircraft scheme. Only a handful of Phantom II units, including VMFA-321 'Hell's Angels' and VF-202 'Superheats', used white codes for a brief three years between 1978 and 1981.

One aspect of this aircraft's 'dress' shows the squadron's contempt for the then new low-viz ruling - the pilot's patriotic bonedome, which was probably a much cherished souvenir from the Bicentennial celebrations.

No less than six (five frontline and one reserve) Corps squadrons entered the 1980s flying unmodified F-4Js passed on to them by the Navy following the arrival of the F-14 in the mid-1970s. All of these units eventually retired the Juliets and re-equipped with S-models. This particular airframe stayed with VMFA-115 until their transition onto the F-4S in 1982, after which it served with fellow Beaufort-based squadron VMFA-122 'Crusaders', before finally being sent to AMARC on 26 April 1985.

Like several other fighter attack units in today's Marine Corps, the 'Silver Eagles' were formed during World War 2. Initially

designated VMF-115, the squadron was commissioned at Santa Barbara, California, on early model F4U Corsairs in July 1943. Winning battle honours across the Pacific, VMF-115 was still equipped with the tough Chance-Vought fighter at the cessation of hostilities. The first unit in the Corps to receive jets, the 'Silver Eagles' took delivery of factory-fresh F9F Panthers direct from Grumman in New York in August 1949. The squadron moved to Yompo, North Korea, the following year to fly strike sorties in support of UN troops. Later in the decade the all-weather F4D-1 Skyray was issued to the 'Silver Eagles', the unit changing their designation to VMF(AW)-115 to better reflect their new role.

The first F-4Bs arrived at Beaufort for the redesignated VMFA-115 in January 1964, and following 12 months of work-ups the unit headed west for Vietnam. After flying a record 35,000 combat sorties, the squadron was stood down and sent to MCAS Iwakuni. Recharged and ready to join the fray once more, VMFA-115 was initially sent back to Chu Lai in August 1970, before moving to Nam Phong, Thailand, in late 1971, and eventually being cycled back to Iwakuni. Transitioning to the F-4J in August 1975, the 'Silver Eagles' finally returned to Beaufort in June 1977 following a 12-year stint overseas. In their last year with the Juliet model, VMFA-115 participated in USS *Forrestal's* (CV-59) 1981 Mediterranean cruise, receiving the F-4S soon after their return to Beaufort. By December 1984 all the Phantom IIs had gone from the squadron ramp, and on 3 July 1985 VMFA-115 rather fittingly became the inaugural F/A-18 unit within MAG-31.

Streaming its drogue chute following a successful recovery at El Toro in November 1981, F-4N BuNo 151007 belongs to VMFA-531 'Gray Ghosts', one of the most famous USMC Phantom II operators. When the squadron received their first F4H-1s at Oceana on 31 July 1962 they were based at Cherry Point. The first East Coast unit to be equipped with the new Phantom IIs, VMF(AW)-531, as they were then designated, had barely been declared operational when they were sent south to Key West to perform strip alert duty following the Cuban Missile Crisis of October 1962. During the squadron's six-month stay in Florida they actually went 'head-to-head' with Cuban MiG-17s on one occasion 50 miles south of Key West. It was during this inconclusive engagement that American pilots were first

subjected to the diminutive *Fresco's* legendary short turn radius, a trait that was thoroughly exploited by North Vietnamese Air Force pilots throughout the conflict in Southeast Asia.

Following a WestPac deployment to MCAS Atsugi, Japan, in 1964, the squadron was sent to Da Nang in April 1965, thus becoming the first USMC fixed-wing unit to see action over Vietnam. The 'Gray Ghosts' traded up to the F-4N in 1975, before receiving the potent new F/A-18 in 1983. The USMC's 1991 rationalization program saw VMFA-531 decommissioned as part of MAG-11 on 31 March 1992, and its Hornets passed on to the Marine reserve. This particular F-4N is currently held in the storage facility at Point Mugu awaiting drone conversion.

Several dedicated Phantom II training units were established by the Navy and Marines to ensure that a steady flow of suitably equipped pilots, RIOs and maintainers joined frontline squadrons on both coasts, VF-101 and -121 being commissioned to introduce the F4H-1 into squadron service. For almost a decade Navy instructors taught Marine Corps crews the art of flying the Phantom II, 'leathernecks' being streamed into classes alongside their 'brown shoe' brethren straight out of 'CNATRA (Chief of Naval Air Training) school'. With the escalation of the conflict in Southeast Asia the demand for pilots and RIOs placed too great a strain on the Replacement Air Group units, and two separate Marine Corps F-4 training squadrons were established on either coast.

The first to be commissioned was the F-4B-equipped VMFAT-201 at Cherry Point in 1967, followed two years later by VMFAT-101 at El Toro; they received F-4Js. The former unit's operational life lasted but two years, the Corps' need for fresh crews subsiding as the bombing halt in Vietnam took effect. The 'Sharpshooters' at El Toro (and later Yuma, Arizona) eventually outlasted the Navy training units by over a decade, re-equipping with the November and Sierra models in 1976 and 1982 respectively. The following year VMFAT-101 entered the record books by operating no less than three different types of Navy Phantom II at the same time - the F-4J, N and S! By the end of 1983, however, only the recently received Sierra models still wore the unit's 'SH' tail codes. Looking suitably weathered following many hundreds of hours pounding the circuit over El Toro, BuNo 157254 taxies out in the mid-afternoon sun in August 1982 at the start of yet another mission.

Like most other fleet and frontline replacement squadrons charged with training 'nugget' crews, VMFAT-101's syllabus usually lasted between six and eight months per course, the pilot and RIO being instructed in the basics of flying, VMFA-style. The course would emphasize close air support techniques as well as rudimentary dogfighting and missile intercepts. The 'Sharpshooters' graduated their last class in June 1987, this historic event being followed by the retirement of the squadron's remaining F-4Ss to the nearby AMARC facility at Tucson. BuNo 157254 stayed with VMFAT-101 until the unit's re-equipment with Hornets, the veteran Phantom II arriving for storage on 9 July 1987 along with nine other F-4s. By this stage in its life the aircraft's overall light gray scheme, with full-color national insignia and black titling, had been replaced by TPS grays overall.

15

Dramatically framed by the squadron hangar, this 'cowboy' is packing something a little more potent than a Colt Peacemaker. Armed up with an assortment of weapons that emphasizes the true multi-role capability of the venerable Phantom II, BuNo 155847 is carrying a quartet of Rockeye II cluster bomb units (CBUs) on the inner pylons, three inert Mk 82 low-drag 'iron bombs' on a triple ejector rack fitted to the port outer weapons hardpoint, four drill-round AIM-9Ls on the twin Sidewinder rails and an equal number of AIM-7M Sparrows recessed in their dedicated underbelly troughs. As impressive as this load may look, the unfortunate pilot of 'Cowboy 07' wouldn't get much further than the city limits and back with this configuration. During Vietnam the F-4 generally went to war toting weapons on the inner pylons, and either a single large (600 US gal) external tank on the centerline, or a pair of smaller (370 US gal) ones on the outer hard points. A mix of bombs, CBUs, missiles and unguided rockets could be chosen, depending on the mission tasking. The distinctive shading between the three TPS grays is clearly visible in this evenly lit photograph, as is the scheme's susceptibility to weathering. One of the more obvious external features of the F-4S are the thin USAF-style formation strips fitted in strategic locations on the fuselage and fin.

(Right) Looking far less warlike than their overburdened compadre, a fighting pair of F-4Ss from VMFA-112 head back to Dallas after successfully expending their 25 lb Mk 76 'blue bombs' on the local weapons range. These inert devices fit straight onto the modified TERs affixed to the inner missile pylons, and accurately simulate the ballistics of a 500 lb Mk 82 SE Snakeye retarded weapon. The lead jet is also carrying an AIM-9 acquisition round for air combat training, this device providing the crew with the lock-on solution and 'growl' of the real thing without the actual Sidewinder bite. Prior to the advent of the F-4S, and with it the arrival of TPS grays, VMFA-112's Phantom IIs wore a smart navy blue band adorned with five white stars across their fins.

(Right) Breaking hard to starboard away from the cameraship, a weathered F-4S, stained by fluid leaks, shows off its extended slats and centerline tank prior to returning to NAS Dallas in February 1991. Similarly configured is 153792, the oldest and most senior of VMFA-112's 14-strong Phantom II fleet. As a result of its stately age this airframe was officially designated the 'boss bird' of the squadron - it wore both the '00' modex and the name of Col.Ken W.Dewey (MAG-41's commanding officer) until the Phantom IIs were retired on 18 January 1992. The bulges on the intakes of all the F-4Ss featured in this volume contained Sanders AN/ALQ-126 antennas for the aircraft's Deceptive Electronic Counter Measures system.

One of the first units commissioned after Pearl Harbour, VMF-112 fought across the Pacific in all the major campaigns; their involvement in the thick of the action resulted in them scoring the third highest number of kills for a Marine squadron during World War 2. Recommissioned with the FG-1D Corsair in 1946, the squadron was assigned to the reserves. Flying a multitude of types over the years, VMF(AW)-112 entered the 1970s equipped with F-8A Crusaders. F-4Ns replaced the venerable Vought fighters in 1976, the Novembers in turn making way for Juliet models in 1983. After a solitary year with the F-4J, a surplus of ex-US Navy F-4Ss allowed VMFA-112 to retire its unmodified Phantom IIs at roughly the same time as its frontline contemporaries at Beaufort.

NAS Dallas earned itself the reputation as the final home for operational F-4Ss in the mid- to late 1980s, the two US Navy Reserve and single Marine Reserve squadrons at the Texas facility having a virtual monopoly on the premier nautical Phantom II in its last years of service to the nation. The first of the trio to relinquish its ties with the 'St Louis Slugger' was VF-201 'Hunters', the unit flying its last F-4S to AMARC in December 1986, an event that was followed in the New Year by the arrival of the first F-14. This particular re-manufactured F-4J actually returned to sea prior to its eventual retirement on 21 November 1986, participating in VF-161 'Chargers' last WestPac with the Phantom II aboard the USS *Midway* (CV-41) as 'Rock River 103'. Photographed on short finals to Dallas in March 1985, BuNo 153859 wears a period TPS color scheme, brightened only by the addition of two yellow bonedomes poking up above the canopy sill.

The F-4S was still a capable dogfighter even into its twilight years, thanks in no small part to the enlarged leading-edge slats retrofitted to the wings during the major upgrade. Clearly visible in the extended position in this photograph, the slats increased the hulking S-model's combat turn capability by 50 per cent over the F-4J, and allowed the pilot to control the aircraft more precisely in the crucial moments just prior to landing. The slats would normally operate automatically as the aircraft's angle of attack increased, extending at 11.5 units of AOA, and retracting at 10.5 units. The slats could also be manually overridden from the cockpit. VF-201, and fellow Reserve Carrier Air Wing 20 members VF-202 'Superheats', were initially formed on the F-8H Crusader at Dallas on 25 July 1970. Freshly refurbished F-4Ns replaced the decidedly mature Crusaders four years later, the squadron flying garishly marked November models up until February 1984 when the ultimate Navy Phantom II arrived at Dallas. Today, there is still an F-4 waving the McAir fighter flag in 'Grumman country' at Dallas: F-4N BuNo 152267 proudly guards the main gate wearing full pre-TPS VF-201 colors.

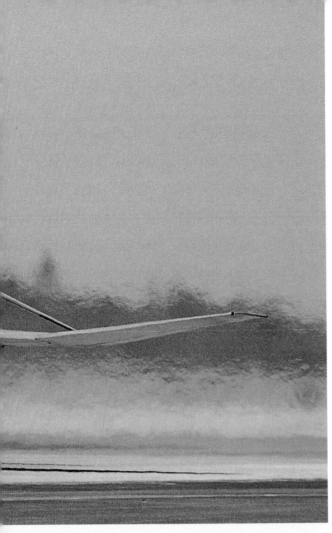

Aside from the dozen short-lived (designationwise, at least) F-4G data link Phantom IIs that served with VF-213 'Black Lions' between 1964 and 66, the rarest of the breed to don a suit of nautical gray was the RF-4B, a mere 46 of which were built for the Marine Corps in two batches. With the engines spooled up and the brakes firmly applied, BuNo 151980 prepares to roll down the long El Toro runway at the start of yet another training sortie. Photographed in August 1985, this veteran had celebrated its 20th birthday the previous month, McAir article 968 having performed its first flight at Lambert Field on 23 July 1965. Following sterling service with the Corps over Vietnam, this airframe (plus four other early-build RF-4Bs) spent two and a half years stored at Davis-Monthan between December 1970 and June 1972.

Overhauled following its sojourn in the Arizona desert, BuNo 151980 was issued firstly to VMCJ-3 at El Toro, and then absorbed into the newly formed VMFP-3 on 1 July 1975 when the latter unit took control of all three composite reconnaissance squadrons. Well equipped for the tactical recce role, the RF-4B used optical, infrared and electronic sensors to perform its mission 24 hours a day, in any weather. As is always the case with Marine equipment, the recce-Phantom II was forced to serve a lot longer than was originally planned, and in 1978 an extensive overhaul program was instigated at the North Island NARF. Titled Project SURE (Sensor Update and Refurbishment Effort), the rework included the installation of an AN/ASN-92(V) Carrier Alignment Inertial Navigation system, AN/ASW-25B Datalink, AN/AAD-5 Infrared Reconnaissance Set, AN/APD-10 Sideways-Looking Airborne Radar (SLAR) and an AN/AP- 202 Radar Beacon. The airframe was also thoroughly gutted and rewired, and new J79s fitted. Following its 'face lift' in San Diego, BuNo 151980 continued to serve with VMFP-3 until it was despatched to AMARC on 12 July 1989, joining 15 other RF-4Bs retired in that same year.

To mark the phase-out of the RF-4B and the disbandment of VMFP- 3, the 'boss bird' of the unit was resprayed in overall gloss gray, and given a stunning fin decoration which reflected the traditional CAG colors worn by nautical Phantom IIs in the 1960s and 70s. Flanked by USMC reconnaissance platforms from the past (F9F-8P Cougar) and the future (F/A-18D Hornet), this veteran was the first RF-4B built in the second batch of ten recce-Phantom IIs ordered by the Corps; these aircraft differed from the first batch because they actually married an RF-4C fuselage with F-4J wings. Test flown on 2 April 1970, the aircraft initially served with VMCJ-2 'Playboys' at Cherry Point before joining VMFP-3 in 1975.

Three distinct composite squadrons (VMCJ-1, -2 and -3) had, up to that point, operated the Phantom IIs alongside the Corps' handful of EA-6A 'Electric' Intruders at Iwakuni, Cherry Point and El Toro. Following a temporary re-organization during exercise Solid Shield, it was found that two units at full squadron strength could more effectively control the reconnaissance and electronic warfare elements of the Marine Air force. Thus VMFP-3 'Specters' (latterly known as 'Rhinos', due to their callsign) and VMAQ-2 'Playboys' were born, based at El Toro and Cherry Point respectively. Although the parent organization was based in California, VMFP-3 continued to fulfil various tactical responsibilities by deploying flights of three or four aircraft to MAG-12 at Iwakuni and MAG-24 at Kaneohe Bay, in Hawaii, as well as providing aircraft and crews for WestPac deployments aboard the *Midway* up until 1984. Equipped with 21 operational RF-4Bs at their peak, the 'Specters' carried out their own conversion training onto type throughout the 1980s. When the unit deactivated on 10 August 1990 the five remaining Phantom II's were flown cross-country to Cherry Point for parts reclamation and eventual storage at the base's NARF facility.

Silver Wings

Although the Navy and Marines were the first into Phantom IIs, the US Air Force held onto their F-4s longer than their nautical counterparts. If you wanted to pick one typically high time 'Rhino' at random to illustrate the varied operational history of the Phantom II in USAF service, then look no further than F-4D-31-MC 66-7771. Apart from the odd fleck of paint missing around the serial on the fin, this veteran looks as fresh as the day it was delivered to the 432nd Tactical Reconnaissance Wing (TRW) at Udorn Royal Thai Air Force Base (RTAFB) shortly after leaving the McDonnell Douglas factory in 1967. Although its wing mates were responsible for the destruction of no less than 35 NVAF MiGs between 1967 and 1973 (for the loss of 12 F-4s), this particular jet never succeeded in achieving a score.

Transferred to the 49th Tactical Fighter Wing (TFW) at Holloman AFB, New Mexico, in early 1970, '771 was allocated to the 9th

Tactical Fighter Squadron (TFS), nicknamed 'The Iron Knights'. Like our weary warrior, the 49th TFW had only recently returned to the USA, having spent its entire 22-year existence up to that point assigned to either the Pacific Air Forces (PACAF-1948/57) or United States Air Forces Europe (USAFE-1957/69). Due to its recent links with Europe the 49th became the first 'dual based' NATO-committed wing in the USAF, organized and trained to re-deploy to Germany at very short notice. As a result of this tasking, the wing staged an annual transatlantic exercise to several USAFE bases under the codename *Crested Cap* - '771 participated in four of the first six such exercises, flying from Hahn and Bitburg on various deployments. In between *Crested Cap III* and *IV*, the 49th TFW was sent to Takhli RTAFB on 7 May 1972 for a four-month long combat tour.

Still part of the 9th TFS, '771 was once again bombed up and

sent east to destroy 'strategic' targets in both North and South Vietnam. Following its participation in *Crested Cap VIII*, the aircraft was sent to Hill AFB for overhaul in October 1976, and then issued to the 474th TFW at Nellis AFB, Nevada. This famous wing was then in the process of receiving ex-USAFE F-4Ds from RAF Lakenheath as part of Operation *Ready Switch* - their previous complement of F-111As had been transferred to the 366th TFW at Mountain Home, AFB, Idaho, who in turn had sent their F-111Fs to RAF Lakenheath. Sprayed up in 'NA' codes and decorated with the 430th TPS's red fin cap and canopy rails, '771 was photographed crossing the runway threshold at Nellis in February 1981. Vast numbers of F-16 Fighting Falcons were by this stage flooding out of General Dynamics' Fort Worth plant in Texas, and the 474th relinquished their last F-4Ds only a matter of weeks after this photo was taken.

Resprayed in wraparound tan and two-tone green, '771 was issued to the newly activated, reserve-manned, 89thTFS/906thTFG at Wright-Patterson AFB, Ohio. Maintained in immaculate condition and resprayed in 'Hill Grays' in the mid-1980s, the weary airframe was a regular participant in the biennial *Sentry Wolverine* exercise held at Selfridge ANGB, Michigan, for Guard and Reserve units. With the 89th TFS transitioning to F-16A/Bs in October 1989, it was finally time for 66-7771 to make its last flight to the AMARC facility at Davis-Monthan; this final sortie was duly performed the following month, '771 being accompanied by the unit's 21 other F-4Ds (including '772 and '773).

(Above) Unlike most F-4D-29-MC block aircraft, this heavily weathered 'Rhino' never actually 'loaded out' with ordnance to wage war in Southeast Asia. Fate ordained that 67-483 should spend its service career zooming through the crystalline skies over Edwards AFB as part of the 6512th Test Squadron's large fleet of combat types. No less than 24 Phantom IIs of varying marks were utilized by the Air Force Flight Test Center (AFFTC) over a 29-year period from October 1963 to June 1992, the aircraft performing all manner of tasks ranging from target towing to cruise missile chasing.

Sprayed up in a shade of air superiority gray similar to that worn by Guard interceptor squadrons of the period, '483 was photographed upon arrival at Hill AFB on 11 November 1982, the decidedly weary-looking airframe having been despatched to Utah to be overhauled at the Ogden Air Logistics Center. As with the other Phantom IIs at Edwards, this aircraft was resprayed in an overall gloss white scheme once the rework had been completed, the wingtips and vertical fin being picked out in red as an aid to further visibility. Having amassed a total of 4070 hours flight time in conjunction with various programs, NF-4D 67-483 was finally sold in April 1991 to Tracor Flight Systems Inc of Mojave, California. Placed on the civil register as N430FS, the jet spends its time criss-crossing the country in support of government defense contracts, its now radarless radome serving as a handy compartment in which the crew can store their golf clubs!

Although the groundcrews at the 15th Tactical Reconnaissance Squadron (TRS) were extremely proud of their RF-4Cs, rest assured that this Thunderbirds-style send-off was not routinely performed on a day-to-day basis. The oriental flavour exhibited in the fin markings was also non-standard, a close examination of the Japanese religious symbol giving a clue to the reason behind these theatricals - RAM '86. Held biennially at Bergstrom AFB in Texas, the Reconnaissance Air Meet was essentially the fast jet recce world's *William Tell*. Only the best airframes, air- and groundcrews were sent to RAM, the squadrons choosing their representatives through in-house competitions prior to the 10-day event.

Points were awarded for virtually everything during the exercise, ranging from the actual time of arrival compared to the estimated ETA, through to the appearance of the trio of aircraft sent to compete - after checking out those spotless exhaust nozzles and gleaming tailcone skinning, no judge could possibly award the 15th TRS anything less than full points in the latter competition. Teams from the US Navy, Marine Corps, USAF, ANG and Reserves competed with foreign entries from the Luftwaffe, RAF and RAAF in a total of 19 events. All facets of the reconnaissance mission were examined, including photo interpretation and aircraft maintenance procedures, plus, of course, the flying aspect of the role itself.

Being the only dedicated USAF recce unit in the region, the 15th TRS 'Cotton Pickers' were charged with flying the PACAF flag at both RAM '86 and '88 - the squadron deactivated several months prior to the 1990 event. As USAF squadrons go, the 15th TRS possessed one of the longest traceable histories of any outfit in the force, the 'Cotton Pickers' having originally formed as the 2nd Aviation School Squadron in May 1917. Soon redesignated the 15th Aero Squadron, the fledgling flyers were allocated a mix of

Curtiss JN-4 Jennys and de Havilland DH-9s. Tasked with supporting the Army through aerial observation between the wars, the 15th TRS put this peacetime experience to good use over Europe in 1943-45, flying Mustangs with the 67th Observation Group. Come the jet age the squadron went to war once more, 'Cotton Pickers' RF-86F Sabres performing long range recce missions across North Korea and China.

Following the armistice the 15th TRS moved to Yokota in Japan, trading its war-weary Sabres for RF-84 Thunderflash jets. A further move to Kadena AFB, Okinawa, occurred in 1956, the unit trading up to RF-101 Voodoos two years later. More battle honours were won over Vietnam during 1964-66, the squadron finally taking a well-earned break to transition onto the RF-4C in February 1967. The Phantom II equipped the 15th TRS for an amazing 23 years, the squadron performing all manner of tasks for its immediate controlling body, the Kadena-based 18th TFW, and PACAF units in general. Regular detachments operated from several locations across Southeast Asia, the squadron's small facility at Taegu, South Korea, eventually being expanded in October 1989 to house the 15th TRS lock, stock and barrel as part of a re-organization program at Kadena.

Assigned to the 51st TFW/460th TRG, the 'Cotton Pickers' sojourn in Korea was brief: the unit was deactivated in the spring of 1990, and its 16 RF-4s sent back to the US, or sold to the Republic of Korea Air Force. This aircraft was destined never to fly again, however, the once pristine 68-551 having 'life exed' its airframe by this point - its sensor equipment and wings parted company with the fuselage and were MAC-flighted back to America. The remaining torso was passed onto the Koreans at Taegu, who used it for aircraft battle damage repair. How could they bring themselves to perform such a heinous act?

Prior to the first RAM (held in November 1986), the major exercise for CONUS-based recce assets was *Photo Finish*, a competition which pitted the seven Air National Guard (ANG) RF-4 squadrons against a pair of similarly equipped Air Force units. Held annually at various Guard bases, the exercise was structured along similar lines to the appreciably larger RAM. In 1985, one of the participating USAF units was the 16th TRS from Shaw AFB, South Carolina. The only non-F-16 squadron in the 363rd TFW, the 16th TRS was at that point the most experienced RF-4 outfit in existence; the first group of recce Phantom II aircrew had commenced training with the 363rd TRW's (as it was then designated) 4415th Combat Crew Training Squadron at Shaw AFB on 19 January 1965. Ten months later these same pilots and weapons systems officers were flying combat sorties with the 2nd Air Division over the jungles of Vietnam.

Postwar, the wing's numerical strength peaked at the end of the 1970s, the 363rd TRW controlling three TRSs (16th, 18th and 62nd) and a single training squadron (33rd TRTS). In April 1982 the F-16A arrived at Shaw, and at the end of the transitory phase only the 16th TRS remained equipped with 28 RF-4Cs. Redesignated a tactical fighter wing at the same time, the 363rd was assigned to the USAF's Rapid Deployment Force. Prior to this new tasking, the 16th TRS had regularly deployed to Europe throughout the 1970s during *Salty Bee* exercises, the 363rd TRW alternating their participation in this recce-optimized event with the Bergstrom-based 67th TRW. 67-464 participated in the 1982 and 86 deployments, both of which took place at RAF Alconbury in Suffolk.

Photographed passing through Hill AFB on 8 October 1985, 67-464 still looked resplendent in its freshly applied 'Europe One' charcoal gray and two-tone green scheme and detailed squadron markings, all of which were sprayed on specially for the unit's participation in that year's *Photo Finish*. As a result of the many hours spent preparing the airframe, the squadron's maintenance department, the 16th AMU, won the award for the best presented RF-4, as denoted by the star spangled figure '1' on the rudder. The squadron was deactivated in late 1989, and although several of the unit's fresher aircraft were passed on to the recently stood-down 67th TRW (September 1992 disestablished), this airframe joined the majority of the other 16th TRS RF-4Cs in storage.

Operating in excess of 3000 combat aircraft of differing ages and types across the world, the USAF fights a constant battle keeping its squadrons equipped with up-to-date and reliable hardware. In order to keep its fleet in peak condition a series of five Air Logistics Centers were set up in the 1960s to overhaul and update frontline, Guard and Reserve aircraft. Each facility specializes in different airframes, the Ogden ALC, for example, focusing purely on the F-4 and its successor, the F-16. Over the decades every surviving Phantom II in USAF service will have made several trips to Utah (the F-4 was slated for a period of deep maintenance every 54 months), the aircraft being stripped back to components and rebuilt by a team of technicians from the Air Force and McDonnell Douglas.

One aircraft that arrived at Hill AFB in the early 1970s and never left was F-4E 68-0304, the second airframe built as part of the largest single Echo model block (245 airframes) ordered by the USAF. Several Phantom IIs of varying marks (F-4C 64-0664 is parked in the background) were retained by the ALC for trials work and communication flights. Wearing a similar scheme to the Edwards fleet, this pristine 'Rhino' was photographed in July 1982 undergoing drag chute checks prior to flying a sortie out of Hill. By the look of the gravitational pull being exerted on the McAir technician's trousers, perhaps he too should be issued with a G-suit. . .

The 'Wild Weasel' mission is by definition one of the most dangerous, yet vital, undertakings assigned to any unit within the USAF. Over the years both the F-105 Thunderchief and F-4 Phantom II have heavily contributed to the fulfilment of this mission, both types being linked through a shared history of 'SAM busting' in two deadly conflicts. Photographed taxying out on yet another *Red Flag* mission at Nellis in August 1983, F-4G 69-7216 motors past the decidedly veteran F-105Ds of the reserve-manned 466th TFS/419th TFW, who were also on a det to Nevada from Hill AFB. To further enhance its already impressive ECM suite, 69-7216 has a Westinghouse ALQ-119(V)17 noise/deceptor jammer bolted into the port forward Sparrow trough. At the time this device was state-of-the-art; but when the aircraft deployed to Sheikh Isa airfield in Bahrain with 23 other George-based F-4Gs as part of the wing's contribution to *Desert Storm* seven years later, it carried a more capable Raytheon-mod AN/ALQ-184 pod in its place. Adapted from the ALQ-119, the newer system incorporates a Rotman lens which 'cranks up' the Effective Radiated Power of the pod by a factor of ten!

To return to Nellis AFB: the Phantom II's red AN/APR-47 radar warning receiver housing perched atop the fin denotes that the jet belonged to the 563rd TFS, nicknamed the 'Aces', who were at the time one of three squadrons controlled by the 37th TFW. During its time at George the aircraft regularly participated in *Red Flag* exercises, as the wing was often called upon to ply its specialized trade over the electronic ranges in support of various Allied strike forces. Very early in its history with the 37th TFW, 69-7216 also deployed to RAF Wildenrath in Germany, (along with 11 other F-4Gs) as part of the 563rd TFS's contribution to Exercise *Coronet Fleet*, held in September 1981. When the 37th moved out of George in 1989 and headed east for Tonopah Test Range, and the F-117, the 563rd TFS was deactivated and its F-4Gs split between the re-assigned 561st TFS and the 562nd TFTS, who were absorbed into the 35th TFW. By the time the wing received the word to head east for Bahrain on 15 August 1990 as part of the *Desert Shield* build-up 69-7216 was wearing the yellow fin cap of the 561st TFS 'Black Knights' applied to an overall 'Hill Gray' scheme.

(Left) The home of the largest concentration of F-4s in the type's twilight years in USAF service was George AFB, California. Two wings were based there as part of the 12th Air Force, operating a mixed fleet of F-4E and G-model Phantom IIs. The 35th TFTW (F-4Es) conducted conversion training for the 37th TFW at the base, the former wing also performing transitional work for the Luftwaffe as well - the Germans owned and maintained a flight of eight F-4Es at George specifically for this task. Always maintained in showroom condition, the 35th TFTW's Phantom IIs were split between two squadrons: the 20th and 21st TFTSs. After many years of service, and several different camouflage schemes, F-4Es 67-265 and -266 ended their days with the former unit wearing the fashionable 'Hill Gray' scheme developed in the late 1980s at the Ogden ALC.

Seen here departing on a routine ACM sortie from George in September 1989, the lead 'Lobo' in this two-ship formation was tragically involved in a mid-air collision during a similar flight on 26 July 1990. Accompanying '266 on the fateful mission was Luftwaffe F-4E 75-0630. Practising basic dogfighting over the Furnace Creek area of Death Valley, the two F-4s collided and

crashed. Fortunately two crewmen managed to eject safely from one of the stricken jets, but the other pair were killed in the initial impact.

The 35th Fighter Wing was originally activated at Johnson AFB, Japan, in August 1948, and issued with F-51 Mustangs. Redesignated the 35th Fighter Interceptor Wing in January 1950, the group spent the next seven years moving between bases in Japan and Korea, flying the F-80, F-94 and finally the F-86. Inactivated in October 1957, the wing was reformed at Da Nang AFB in April 1966 and equipped with F-4Cs. Briefly deactivated again in July 1971, the 35th TFW was moved to George three months later. From 1973 to 1980 the wing operated a mix force of F-4s and F-105G 'Wild Weasels'. Redesignated again in July 1984, the outfit spent the next five years as an F-4E/G training wing, before again reverting simply to the 35th TFW in October 1989. Eventually the operation at George wound down, and the last three F-4Gs departed the base on 30 June 1992. The facility itself was closed six months later, and the 35th Wing title itself was moved to Keflavik, Iceland, although the organization at present has no aircraft assigned to it.

A total of 118 'Wild Weasel V' conversion kits were produced by McDonnell Douglas in the mid-1970s, the factory modifying the first two F-4Es at St Louis, with the balance of 114 airframes being upgraded at the Ogden ALC; of the two remaining kits, Nos 1 and 27 were used on the prototype airframe 69-7254 to bring it up to operational specs, while No 89 was never installed for some reason. An average of 14,420 manhours was spent converting an Echo to Golf configuration, the work being spread over 110 days at a cost of $28 million per airframe - the self-same amount charged by McDonnell Douglas back in fiscal year 1969 for a brand new F-4E!

The F-4G's primary function is to seek out and destroy enemy radar sites, particularly when those sites control a surface-to-air missile battery. Initially, the brain of the 'Wild Weasel' was the McDonnell Douglas/Loral-designed AN/APR-38 Radar Warning and Attack system. Built around a Texas Instruments computer, the AN/APR-38 utilized no less than 52 antennas distributed all over the aircraft's fuselage. Signals picked up by antennas were fed to an IBM receiver which passed them on to the computer itself. These signals were threat graded and displayed on a Loral control indicator, the pilot and EWO accessing this information through the Plan Position Indicator, Panoramic and Analysis Display and Homing and Attack scopes. The AN/APR-38 was originally programmed to pick up and prioritize threats at distances of five, ten or 15 miles, but this capability has been drastically improved through the introduction of the Unisys-developed Weasel Attack Signal Processor (WASP). Designated the AN/APR-47 and capable of prioritizing signals eight times faster than the older system, it was fitted to surviving F-4Gs as part of the Performance Update Program (PUP) initiated in the mid 1980s.

Canopies cracked open in an effort to improve the cockpit circulation in the stifling California heat, a quartet of 363rd TFS 'Weasels' roll out to the last chance point prior to launching on a suppression sortie over the Tonopah EW practice range. Photographed on 26 June 1986, all four jets are equipped with AGM-65D Maverick infrared imaging missiles, fitted with active seeker heads but no explosive charge or rocket motors. The 35th TFW's large fleet of F-4Gs (plus some from the 3rd TFW in the Philippines) was due to be split between Idaho and Nevada Air Guard units in 1991/92. However, due to a change in funding only the 124th FG at Gowan Field, Boise, Indiana, received 'Wild Weasels'; this unit, and the active duty 52nd FW at Spangdahlem, Germany, are the last operators of the F-4G.

(Right) Looking for trouble, a mixed four-ship of Echos and Golfs rolls out into the Nevada heat haze, their 'Europe One' matt camo absorbing the sun's rays. From this unusual angle the wing leading-edge slats are clearly visible, the rear edge of these retrofitted lift devices sitting above the flying surface itself. The powerful 'blown' flaps on the inner trailing edges are also apparent, fully drooped and ready for retraction once the aircraft line up on the runway. Photographed in March 1985, the F-4Es hailed from the 35th TFW and the F-4Gs from the 37th TFW. The latter outfit can trace its history back to April 1953 and its premature activation as the 37th Fighter Bomber Wing at Clovis AFB, New Mexico; devoid of aircraft, the unit was stood down two months later. Fourteen years were to elapse before the wing was activated again, although this time they were to last a little longer than 60 days. Formed on F-100Fs at Phu Cat AB in South Vietnam, the 37th TFW performed Forward Air Control (FAC) missions between 1967 and 69. The weary Super Sabres were then replaced by firstly F-4Ds, and then Es, with the wing eventually being sent to George. There it stayed until its previously detailed move to Tonopah.

ANG and AFRES

Following 15 years of frontline service that saw the F-4C take the fight to the NVAF in Southeast Asia, and defend Europe at the height of the Cold War, the well-used 'Charlies' were passed on to the Air National Guard, who in turn used them initially in the fighter interceptor role. The first unit to retire the elegant F-106 Delta Dart in favour of the Phantom II was the 171st Fighter Interceptor Squadron (FIS), who accepted F-4Cs in the spring of 1978. Based at Selfridge Air National Guard Base in Michigan, and controlled by the 191st Fighter Interceptor Group (FIG), the squadron maintained its tradition of decorating its jets in garish black and gold chequers - the end result was arguably the most attractive group of Phantom IIs ever to grace a flightline.

As can be seen from this photograph taken on 6 May 1986, the 171st FIS even produced matching bonedomes for its aircrew. The traditional air superiority gloss gray so long associated with the former Air Defense Command (ADC) helped to hide the age of the unit's 21 F-4Cs, all of which had celebrated their 21st birthdays by the time of their retirement in 1986. One of the oldest of the bunch was 63-7460, built as part of the second batch (F-4C-17-MC) delivered to the USAF in 1965. Despite its advanced years this jet was passed onto the 114th Tactical Fighter Training Squdron at Kingsley Field, Oregon, upon the 171st FIS's re-equipment with F-4Ds. There it swapped its glossy colors for a coat of lustreless tactical 'Hill Grays', before eventually being retired to AMARC in early 1989.

(Below) Not exactly ideal conditions for exposing rolls of Kodachrome 64. Having completed the scheduled long range interception exercises, a pair of 171st FIS F-4Ds let down through the murk prior to breaking out of the overcast and recovering at Selfridge in December 1989. The unit received two dozen slightly less used Deltas to replace the Charlies, following the latter's retirement to Davis-Monthan, in the summer of 1986. During the unit's last 18 months with the Phantom II the distinctive gold and black chequers and chevrons were replaced by 'Hill Grays', although the 171st FIS still managed to pick out the former detailing with the darker shade of the new scheme.

Celebrating their 45th year within the Guard in 1993, the unit's history can be traced back even further to World War 2 and the Eighth Air Force's 374th Fighter Squadron (FS). Renumbered the 107th FS and reassigned to the ANG on 25 April 1948, the squadron flew its first sorties with its recently acquired F-51Ds from Detroit-Mayne Major Airport soon after. Equipped with F-84B Thunderjets and called to active duty as part of the Korean War mobilization in 1950, the squadron was sent to Luke AFB, Arizona, to train pilots converting onto the Republic fighter prior to be sent overseas. Back in Michigan by 1952, the unit's third and final redesignation to the 171st FIS coincided with the brief return of the Mustang, this time the F-51H model. War-surplus F-86Es eventually arrived in Michigan 12 months later, this re-equipment bringing a change in mission; the unit was now charged with air defense duties. Its ability to perform this duty was further enhanced in June 1955 when all-weather F-89C Scorpions replaced the fair-weather Sabres.

Both the squadron's role and designation changed with the arrival in February 1958 of their next combat type, the RF-84F Thunderflash. The rugged Republic recce aircraft put in 13 years of service with the 171st TRS, before being replaced by the equally masculine RF-101A/C Voodoo in January 1971; the squadron moved to Selfridge as part of the transition. The reconnaissance connection was severed just over 12 months later when the most elegant of all the 'century series' fighters, the F-106, was phased in, resulting in the unit being redesignated the 171st FIS once again. During its six-year association with the Delta Dart, the squadron established a Zulu alert detachment in defense of Seymour Johnson AFB, North Carolina, a commitment it still fulfills today with its Air Defense Fighter (ADF) F-16A Fighting Falcons.

(Right) Power personified, a 'Hill Gray' F-4D rolls past a fatigued marshaller towards the runway at Niagara Falls International Airport in upstate New York. Visible on the starboard LAU-105 weapons pylon are two AIM-9L Sidewinders, and beneath the fuselage is the ubiquitous 600-US gal external tank. This particular Delta has had its radar warning receiver system upgraded, additional antennas being fitted beneath the black blisters clustered on the APR-26 RHAW radome housing. To help the pilot keep his 'six' (tail) clear, three rear-view mirrors have been securely fastened to the canopy rail. Wearing the subdued colors of the 136th FIS when photographed in May 1989, 65-0692 was nearing the end of its operational career with the USAF. As with most other ANG Phantom II units, the 136th FIS replaced its aircraft with F-16s during the summer of 1990. Due to its high flying hours, this airframe (along with two other squadron mates) was sent to Davis-Monthan almost a year before the unit's remaining F-4s.

Aside from conventional ACM and beyond visual range (BVR) interception exercises, the interceptor squadrons would also periodically carry out air-to-air gunnery sorties on towed targets. As the early model Phantom IIs were built without internal cannon armament, the many ANG units equipped with F-4Cs and Ds had to resort to the bulky General Electric SUU-23/A centerline pod, which housed a gas-operated GAU-4 20mm cannon and 1200 rounds of ammunition. Those shells were usually fired at a TDU-10B towed target identical to the one being deployed behind the F-4D featured in these photographs. Attached to an RMU-10/A reel pod, which was in turn bolted onto the aircraft's outer weapons pylon, the dart-like target could be trailed up to 5000 ft behind the Phantom II. Attacking jets would make strafing passes from abeam or from the forward quarters of the towing aircraft. The original centerline pod, the SUU-16, had been developed essentially for close air support work over the jungles of Vietnam. However, as missed MiG kills began to mount up through malfunctioning missiles and the lack of an internal gun, so enterprising fighter wings in Southeast Asia began to wage war against the NVAF with the external cannon pod.

Both F-4Ds belong to the 179th FIS of the Minnesota ANG, based at Duluth International Airport, and both completed their 20+ years of service in Air Force ranks with this squadron - 64-980 was actually the last of 52 airframes built in the first batch of Deltas delivered to the USAF back in 1966. The other aircraft featured was part of the huge 320-airframe order of fiscal 1967, many of which ended up in Southeast Asia.

This particular jet, however, went east from St Louis, ending up with the newly re-equipped 48th TFW at RAF Lakenheath. There it stayed until April 1977, when it was transferred back to the US and the 49th TFW. Its stay at Holloman was brief, as the wing soon transitioned onto the F-15 Eagle, and the Phantom II duly moved north to the 474th TFW at Nellis in September 1977. Just under a year later '490 was again transferred, this time to the 31st Tactical Training Wing at Homestead AFB in Florida. Its relegation to ANG ranks occurred in the fall of 1983, following a lengthy spell in the Ogden ALC. Whilst undergoing refurbishment, the aircraft exchanged its Southeast Asian greens, tans and browns for the glossy air superiority gray of the then ADC. Upon completion of the rework it was issued to the recently re-tasked 179th FIS, who 12 months prior had been flying RF-4Cs as the 179th TRS.

The arrival of F-4Ds at Duluth brought the interceptor mission back to the 179th where it belonged, following a seven-year spell performing recce duties with TAC. Able to trace its history back to the 393rd FS, who flew P-38s and P-47s in Europe with the Ninth Air Force during World War 2, the squadron was reactivated, redesignated and assigned to the Minnesota ANG as part of the massive enlargement of the latter organization in 1948. As with 44 other ANG fighter units of the period, the 179th FS (Single Engined) was issued with F-51D Mustangs, a type it plugged on with until the summer of 1954; during this time the squadron spent a 20-month period on active duty during the height of the Korean War crisis.

The 179th truly became an FIS with the introduction of the F-94 Starfire, the unit operating the A, B and C models over a five-year period up to July 1959. Another classic interceptor of the decade, the F-89J Scorpion, was ushered in at Duluth as a replacement for the Starfire, and made way in its turn for the F-102A Delta Dagger in late 1966. The last in the uninterrupted series of classic ADC interceptors to wear the squadron's 'Big Dipper' fin motif was the F-101B Voodoo, which served with the squadron from April 1972 until the arrival of the RF-4Cs in January 1976. Moving forward 14 years, the 179th FIS was one of three interceptor squadrons to trade in its F-4Ds for F-16A ADFs in 1990, the unit's last Phantom IIs departing for AMARC in the winter of that year.

Enduring its last New York winter, 66-7491 climbs away from Niagara Falls Airport and out towards the Great Lakes. All ANG assets are maintained to the highest standards, as this jet proves. The stylized Rhino head on the nose of the Phantom II denotes that this machine was part of the four-aircraft team of 136th FIS jets sent to Tyndall AFB, Florida, for *William Tell '88*, the premier air defense exercise for interceptor squadrons. Built as part of the F-4D-29-MC batch, 66-7491 was initially sent to the 49th TFW at Holloman AFB. Following a lengthy spell in New Mexico, the F-4 was sent north to Nellis (along with over a dozen other ex-49th TFW aircraft) and the 474th TFW in October 1976. 66-7491 spent many hours flying over the *Red Flag* ranges during the next four years, before the arrival of F-16As saw it move to the 31st TFW at Homestead, Florida, in May 1980. Tasked with training novice flight crews in the art of Phantom II operations, TAC style, the jet

was on its way again within six months of its Homestead posting. After a prolonged spell in the Ogden ALC and post-refit storage, 66-7491 was amongst the first batch of F-4Ds issued to the 136th FIS in the mid-1980s.

Known as 'New York's Finest', the 136th FIS have been at Niagara Falls since the autumn of 1950. Like many ANG units the 136th FIS can trace their roots to World War 2, and in particular the Eighth Air Force. Over the years the unit has been associated with some of the finest USAF fighters ever to wear a 'star and

bar', including the F-51H, F- 94B and F-86H. Equipped with F-100Cs throughout the 1960s, the 136th TFS (TAC-gained from 1957 to 1971) flew from from Tuy Ho AFB in South Vietnam between January 1968 and June 1971. Upon their return to New York the unit reverted to interceptor tasks with F-101B/F Voodoos, these eventually being replaced by F-4Cs in November 1981. Deltas followed four years later, to be replaced, as noted earlier, by ADF Fighting Falcons in the summer of 1990.

Once this little lot have been uploaded onto the SUU-23/A-toting Oregon Air Guard F-4C, its pilot should have every ACM eventuality covered! What you see here is a Phantom II fully optimized for the interceptor role, a task which the 123rd FIS have performed since the early 1950s. And those missiles are not practice acquisition rounds, they are the real thing. With the aid of the purpose-built, diesel-powered MJ-1B 'jammer', this pair of experienced tech-sergeants will have the weapons load fitted and primed ready for engine spool-up in under 45 minutes. The larger missiles on the trolley are Raytheon AIM-7F Sparrows, destined

for the purpose-built troughs underneath the F-4's fuselage. The rounds are loaded with two guidance vanes missing, the shark-like fins being bolted on after the missiles are snugged into the troughs. The four Sidewinders sitting above the Sparrows are Ford AIM-9P-3 versions, this model incorporating the improved SR116 rocket motor. The USAF's large stock of AIM-9P-5s consists primarily of rebuilt -9B/E and J model Sidewinders, upgraded ten to twelve years ago.

One of two F-4 units based in Oregon throughout most of the 1980s, the 123rd FIS can trace its roots back to the 123rd

Observation Squadron activated in April 1941. After performing antisubmarine patrols and air support training for ground troops, the unit finally went to war over China as the 35th Photo Reconnaissance Squadron, equipped with F-5 Lightnings. Reorganised and redesignated following VJ-Day, the 123rd FS was issued with P-51Ds. A call to active duty during the Korean War brought with it F-84Cs, although a reversion to ANG controls saw F-51Ds return to Portland Airport. Like most other interceptor units within the ANG, the 123rd FIS flew F-86As, F-94Bs, F-89D/H/ and Js, F-102As and F-101Bs prior to receiving their first F-4Cs .

Following seven years of sterling service with the 'Rhino', the 123rd FIS traded in the ANG's last F-4Cs in the autumn of 1989, receiving second-hand F-15A/Bs from the recently deactivated 318th FIS. Like its fellow ANG interceptor units (12 in total) this squadron is currently threatened with disbandment following the Pentagon's recently tabled Report on the Roles, Missions and Functions of the Armed Forces of the United States, which recommends that this job can be adequately performed by multi-role wings.

With three of the four Sparrows firmly fitted in their fuselage troughs, the two 'teckies' carefully slide the remaining AIM-7 into place. As can be seen from this ramp-level shot, the 'jammer' has been designed to fit easily beneath the wings of most USAF tactical aircraft, thus reducing the amount of back strain inflicted of the line crews. Nicknamed 'Miss Piggy', F-4C 64-0776 was undoubtedly the pick of the 17-strong Phantom II fleet at Portland, having reduced the NVAF's MiG fleet by three during the spring of 1967. Twenty-two years before this photograph was taken, a much younger '776 was to be found sharing revetment space at Da Nang with 72 other F-4Cs from the 366th TFW.

The 'Gunfighters' had been in-theater since March 1966, having initially been based at Phan Rang prior to moving north to replace the battle-weary 35th TFW. This airframe had been delivered new to the 366th TFW in late 1965, the wing passing its F-100s onto the ANG as a steady flow of factory-fresh airframes arrived at Holloman AFB from St Louis; the jet was issued to the 389th TFS, and wearing the colors of this unit it went to war. Tasked primarily with protecting F-105 strike packages, the 366th TFW had enjoyed considerable success over North Vietnam during the Rolling Thunder campaign - the wing was credited with 14 kills, including the first USAF MiG-21 of the war, between April 1966 and June 1967, losing only a single Phantom to the VNAF during the same period. The first of '776's kills was scored on 23 April 1967 by Maj.Robert D.Anderson and Capt.Fred D.Kjer (both of whom were qualified Phantom II pilots) when they downed a MiG-21 south of Hanoi.

Just under a month later the jet was involved in a double MiG kill, this time with Lt.Col.Robert F.Titus and 1st Lt.Milan Zimer up front. This crew had bagged a MiG-21 two days previously in 64-0777 (coincidentally, that jet spent its last years in service as '776's ramp mate at the 123rd FIS). As 'Wander 01', Titus and Zimer were performing an F-105 escort mission similar to that flown on 20 May, their target this time being railyards west of Hanoi. Running in on the drop zone, the strike package was bounced by a pair of MiG-21s from the nearby Hoa Loc airfield. Sensing trouble even before spotting the enemy fighters, Titus had already punched off his external tanks ready for action. He spotted the MiGs at 12 o'clock and immediately accelerated to engage; but after experiencing clutter trouble with his APQ-100 radar following lock-on, Titus lost contact and returned to the Thunderchiefs.

With the F-105s in sight, he spotted another MiG-21 at six o'clock heading for the bombers at Mach 1+. Titus ordered the F-105s to break just as the enemy fighter loosed off an AA-2 Atoll missile; this failed to guide as the MiG pilot was forced to break off his attack due to Titus and Zimer's manoeuvring. The MiG-21 rapidly climbed towards the overcast above, the small silver fighter entering the cloud base just as Titus fired a Sparrow. The F-4 continued to track the MiG through the cloud deck; but though the missile impacted the Russian jet at the wing root, severing it from the fuselage, Titus and Zimer failed to see the Sparrow hit the MiG. Breaking through the overcast they spotted another fighter which they thought was the same jet. They closed on the second MiG-21 and, following a roller-coaster ride from 25,000 down to 1000 ft, achieved an excellent firing position. Because of the MiG's proximity to the ground the F-4's radar failed to achieve a lock-on, however, and Titus switched to the centerline SUU-16/A gun pod which, rather fortuitously, he was carrying for the first time. After hosing the MiG-21 from stem to stern in a seven-G climb, he was in the process of making a second pass at the seemingly undamaged fighter when the 20mm cannon jammed. With the MiG now apparently out of reach, both Titus and Zimer were stunned to see the pilot totally misjudge his altitude and crash into the northern bank of a river at extremely high speed. The crew only realized they had also downed the first MiG upon rejoining the now egressing F-105s.

(Left) Crews for 'Miss Piggy' and her squadron mates received interceptor training prior to being declared fit for operational flying at the 114th Tactical Fighter Training Squadron (TFTS) - quite why this unit was given a 'Tactical' handle is a mystery, considering that its replacement training unit tasking was for interceptor squadrons only. As with the 123rd FIS, the 114th TFTS was controlled by the 142nd Fighter Interceptor Group, the only FIG in the Guard to have two such units under its command. All pilot and WSO requirements for the seven FISs within the ANG were satisfied by the 114th TFTS, who operated a larger complement of F-4Cs than the other 'frontline' interceptor squadrons from their facility at Kingsley Field in Klamath Falls, Oregon.

One of the oldest Charlie models to carry the unit's distinctive bald eagle emblem on its fin, 63-7428 was photographed in October 1988 cruising past Mt Shasta in northern California on its way back to Oregon following a temporary det to March AFB. Like all other FISs, the unit had long since sprayed over its attractive ADC gloss grays with the flat shades of the 'Hill Gray' scheme by the time this shot was taken - the F-4 was despatched to AMARC less than 12 months later. Activated as recently as 1948, the 114th TFTS was originally formed as a light bomber squadron within the New York ANG, and based at Floyd Bennett Field. Redesignated an interceptor squadron in June 1957, the unit was briefly equipped with the F-94B before being deactivated in September 1958. Thirty-one years later, following a lengthy spell on the F-4C, the 114th TFTS traded up to the F-16 ADF, receiving a mixed fleet of Alpha and Bravo models.

Another unit supplied with aircrew via Oregon was the 178th FIS, the so-called 'Happy Hooligans' of the North Dakota ANG having the distinction of being the first Guard squadron issued with F-4Ds back in March 1977. That same batch of early-build Deltas remained at Hector Field with the squadron for its entire 13-year association with the Phantom II, younger F-4Ds arriving periodically as attrition replacements. Three of the oldest 'Rhinos' at Hector Field are featured sharing ramp space with four camouflaged (and mysteriously unmarked) TAC-assigned F-4Ds on 14 February 1984. These aircraft are equipped with live AIM-7F Sparrows in the traditional missile troughs and all three jets still wear *William Tell* two-digit serials on their rudders. The glossy paint and full unit markings (including an oakleaves citation bar forward of the ANG shield) contrast markedly with the lustreless Southeast Asian tan and green camouflage of the younger F-4Ds. Of the three 178th FIS jets, 64-0939 was the first airframe despatched to Davis-Monthan from North Dakota - it was logged in at the AMARC facility on 10 June 1988.

While equipped with the F-4D the 178th FIS twice deployed overseas on exercise, replacing frontline squadrons that had temporarily returned to the USA. Six Phantom IIs were sent to Keflavik, Iceland, to replace 5th FIS F-4Es that had deployed to Tyndall for a *William Tell* in April 1984; and three F-4Ds were despatched to Ramstein AFB as part of *Creek Klaxon* when the 86th TFW converted from F-4Es to F-16C/Ds in September 1986 - the unit shared Air Defense Alert duties with two other ANG squadrons. In that same year the 'Happy Hooligans' won the F-4D category at *William Tell*, the squadron having been awarded a similar trophy twice before whilst flying F-101Bs in 1970 and 72. Like most other interceptor squadrons the 178th FIS has spent the last 45 years flying a succession of famous fighters, including the F-51D, F-94A/B/C, F-89D/J, F-102A, F-101B, and since 1990, the F-16ADF.

Looking as fresh as the day it left the St Louis factory wearing Southeast Asian tan and greens almost two decades earlier, F-4D 65-0760 nears the end of an 18-month spell at the Ogden ALC on Valentine's Day, 1984 - any ANG crew would have proudly accepted this gleaming beauty as their sweetheart! The 194th FIS at Fresno Air Terminal, California, soon became the lucky guys, adding their familiar blue stripe and 'California' titling to the aircraft's fin. Prior to its ANG days 65-0760 had spent time with the 49th and 31st TFWs, amongst others, deploying on several occasions to Germany with the former as part of the series of *Crested Cap* exercises held annually in the early 1970s. Spared the 'Hill Grays', the aircraft served with the 194th FIS until being retired to AMARC on 23 August 1988, still in its ADC glossy gray. Only the second F-4D despatched to Davis-Monthan from Fresno, 65-0760 was joined by the rest of its former squadron mates the following summer as the 194th FIS transitioned onto the F-16A/B ADF.

Equipped with F-4Ds in late 1983, the squadron maintained a

permanent two-aircraft alert detachment at George AFB throughout the decade, and also sent a trio of jets to Ramstein AB in 1986 for the *Creek Klaxon* deployment. The squadron's history can be traced back to October 1943 and the 409th FS, equipped with P-39s, P-40s and finally P-51s. Based in the US throughout the war providing replacement pilots for European and Pacific theater wings, the squadron was inactivated three months after VJ Day. Coming under ANG control from May 1946, the squadron was not equipped with aircraft until March 1949

when a dozen F-51Ds were issued to the 194th FS at Hayward Municipal Airport. The 'new age' arrived in the shape of T-33s and F-86As in the autumn of 1954, the unit moving to Fresno at the same time due to their former home's unsuitability for jet operations. All weather F-86L 'Sabre Dogs' replaced the Alphas in 1958, these aircraft in turn being phased out in favour of the F-102A in the winter of 1969. After a decade of 'Deuce' flying the 194th traded up to Convair's ultimate Century Series fighter, the simply stunning F-106 Delta Dart.

The Delta model was the most successful 'MiG killer' of the Vietnam conflict, being responsible for 44 confirmed claims between June 1967 and January 1973. As the F-4D was progressivly replaced in frontline service by firstly the F-4E and then the F-16, many 'MiG killers' were transferred to ANG or reserve-manned squadrons. Despite being periodically resprayed in the currently fashionable camouflages, these historically significant aircraft usually retained the traditional red star blazoned on the port splitter plate. Most 'part-time' units could usually boast a single 'MiG killer' within their Phantom II ranks, and occasionally a pilot or WSO on the crew roster. However, in 1987 down at Tinker AFB in Oklahoma it was easier to list the aircraft and crews at the 465th TFS, AFRES, that did *not* have a MiG kill to their credit!

Four F-4Ds wore red stars (although only three had confirmed kills), and two pilots had been involved in successful missions whilst serving as WSOs. The three confirmed jets are photographed here on a specially arranged sortie from Tinker on 23 September 1987. The closest machine, with a glossy AIM-9P on its port pylon, achieved its kill while assigned to the 13th

TFS/432nd TRW. Flown by Capt.Doyle Baker (a USMC exchange pilot) and Lt. John Ryan, this aircraft was credited with downing a MiG-17 while protecting a strike against marshalling yards near Hanoi, the *Fresco* being destroyed by an AIM-7 Sparrow after the pilot had exhausted his gun pod ammmunition during several ineffective passes on the NVAF fighter.

The middle F-4D in this formation bagged a MiG-21 near Hoa Binh on 16 April 1972 whilst on a CAP sortie during the *Linebacker* period. Crewed by Maj.Dan Cherry and WSO ace Capt.Jeff Feinstein, 'Basco 3' was part of a four-ship despatched from Udorn RTAFB by the 13th TFS/432nd TRW to protect a strike force of Phantom IIs from Korat. When the bomb-laden F-4Ds failed to rendezvous on time the CAP force pressed on into North Vietnam by themselves. Equipped with three external tanks, three AIM-7s and two AIM-9s, 'Basco 3's' configuration allowed it to patrol north of the DMZ for quite a time. The flight lead picked up a pair of MiG-21s on radar at 15 miles and steered the quartet into a visual interception position, with the enemy holding the height advantage by about 5000 ft. As the lead pair closed for the kill a third MiG-21 attempted to attack the F-4Ds from a low-level

position. However, he spotted Cherry and Feinstein's jet and flew into cloud in an effort to escape. After spending several minutes fruitlessly sweeping above the cloud bank, Cherry was about to break off and head back down to help out his flight lead when his wingman spotted the NVAF fighter above the Phantom IIs.

Following a series of aggressive manoeuvres, and the judicious use of afterburner, 'Basco 3' finally achieved a solid Sidewinder tone and Cherry pulled the trigger - but the missile failed to fire. After two unsuccessful attempts he relinquished the lead to his wingman, who in turn failed to secure a lock-on for his Sparrows. The pilot, Capt.Greg Crane, nevertheless loosed off a trio of Sparrows using his 'Mk1 eyeball' for guidance. The third round just failed to hit the target, the MiG-21 pilot losing all his forward momentum as he broke hard to avoid the missile. With the NVAF fighter now virtually 'dead in the air', Cherry moved past Crane in full afterburner and loosed off a locked-up Sparrow from the MiG-21's six o'clock. The missile tracked as advertised and knocked the fighter's wing off.

The furthest 'Okie' in this formation was in fact the first of the trio to claim a kill, its MiG-21 victory on 24 October 1967 being only the second aircraft downed by the then new F-4D version of the Phantom II. Assigned to the legendary 8th TFW 'Wolfpack' at Ubon, the aircraft wore the colors of the 433rd TFS (this victory was the unit's tenth kill and the wing's 25th), and was flown by Maj.William L.Kirk and 1st Lt.Theodore R.Bongartz. This was Kirk's second kill of the war; he had already claimed a MiG-17 on 13 May 1967 whilst flying an F-4C with the same squadron. Following its tours of duty in Vietnam 66-7750 served with the 50th TFW at Hahn, the 81st TFW at Bentwaters and the 52nd TFW at Spangdahlem, before returning 'stateside' to the 474th TFW at Nellis in July 1978. Following a long spell at the Ogden ALC the aircraft was issued to the 465th TFS in November 1982; upon its retirement from AFRES service in 1988 it was passed on to the Republic of Korea Air Force along with a handful of other veteran F-4Ds.

(Above) The past and the present perform a joint strike sortie on the Smokie Hill bombing range in Kansas. The F-4D carries the squadron titling on its fin (denoting that it is the CO's machine), whilst the F-16A is marked up with the wing's number. The transition from Phantom II to Fighting Falcon usually took between six and eight months for the ANG and AFRES units, and like most other 'part-time' outfits the 457th TFS received decidedly second-hand F-16As to replace their F-4s.

(Below) In the mid- to late 1960s the sprawling bases in Thailand and South Vietnam heaved with the volume of F-4Ds flying combat sorties across the DMZ into the north. Ten years later CONUS and USAFE facilities boasted the largest numbers of Phantom IIs in the inventory. By the late 1980s only a handful of US bases could boast F-4s in anything larger than squadron strength. One of the last bastions of the Phantom II was McConnell AFB in Kansas, home to the 184th TFG and this pristine F-4D. Tasked with training ANG and AFRES pilots and WSOs in both basic and advanced Phantom II handling skills throughout the 1980s, the group controlled over 50 F-4Ds split between two squadrons. Photographed embarking on a post-overhaul check flight at Hill AFB in February 1982, 66-7459 wears a fresh coat of Southeast Asia camouflage finished off with a period low-viz star and bar - the TAC-assigned ANG and AFRES squadrons adopted 'Europe One' greens and charcoal gray soon after this aircraft had left the ALC.

The 184th TFG had provided replacement crew training on the group's previous type, the F-105D, before receiving F-4Ds in 1979. By the time the last Phantom IIs left McConnell in March 1990 over 1,220 pilots and WSOs had transitioned onto the F-4D during the group's 11-year association with the 'Rhino'. Averaging 9600 training sorties annually, the 'Jayhawks' accrued more F-4D hours than any other group in the Air Force. Not only charged with training ANG and AFRES crews, the 184th TFG also instructed a large number of frontline pilots and WSOs as well. Aside from all the *ab initio* work the group also ran an F-4 Fighter Weapons School through the 125th TFS and 177th TFTS organisation, still training 'part-time' crews today. The 184th TFG now controls a fleet of over 40 F-16C/Ds.

A slick two-ship departs Tinker in June 1988, just four months
before the type's retirement from the 457th TFS. Behind the
thundering 'Rhinos' can be seen a rather crowded flightline full of
E-3 Sentries, owned and operated by the 552nd Airborne Warning
and Control Wing. The F-4's leading edge slats are fully deployed
for take-off, giving the wing as much 'bite' and lift as is
aerodynamically possible at this critical phase in the sortie. The
507th FG is a relative newcomer to USAF ranks, having been
activated at Tinker in May 1972 and equipped with war-weary
F-105Ds. Stood down between March 1973 and October 1975, the
507th eventually passed its knackered Thunderchiefs on to the
AMARC facility in October 1980, receiving F-4Ds from various
frontline wings in due course.

Hill AFB in the spring is a far more hospitable place, as proven by this gloriously warm photograph of a 'naked' F-4D from the 121st TFS, District of Columbia ANG taxying out for a check flight on 5 May 1987. Despite having stripped the airframe back to bare metal, the engineers at Ogden have resisted plunging this 'Rhino' into aluminium anonymity by re-applying its serial and leaving in place the tell-tale stars and blood red fin cap marking worn by several generations of fighters assigned to the 121st TFS. Sixteen months after this photograph was taken a 'fully clothed' 66-7702 deployed with 12 other squadron jets to Keflavik AB in September 1988 for the NATO *Teamwork* exercise.

Its painted radome hints at the shade of its next camouflage scheme - yep, you guessed it, 'Hill Grays'. A closer look at that radome also reveals that the aircraft has experienced an RWR upgrade while in the hands of the Ogden technicians. Unlike other ANG squadrons, which enjoy state/federal status, the 121st TFS has the President as its commander-in-chief rather than a state governor. Initially tasked with observation and liaison duties following its formation on 10 April 1941, the 121st flew Piper L-4s and Stinson L-5s in support of US troops in Algeria, Italy and France during World War 2. Postwar, the squadron was initially equipped with the F-47D, before receiving the F-84C and then the F-94B during its period of active service from February 1951 to 31 October 1952. Like many ANG units reverting to 'part-time' status as the tide of the Korean War turned, the 121st lost its Starfires and received F-51Hs in return.

As the decade progressed at Andrews AFB a succession of jets came and went, the 121st FS operating both the Echo and Hotel models of the F-86 before trading up to its more capable cousin,

the F-100A, in mid-1960. The 1960s saw the unit maintain its North American connection, the 121st TFS being mobilised to active duty during the Berlin Crisis in 1961 and the Pueblo seizure in 1968. Two dozen war-weary Thunderchiefs arrived at Andrews to replace the F-100Cs in 1971, these jets in turn being sent to AMARC a decade later when the 121st TFS traded up to the F-4D. Like most other TAC-gained ANG Phantom II operators, the 121st TFS re-equipped with F-16A/Bs between September 1989 and October 1990.

(Right) The F-4 assumes its most aggressive air from head on, the bulged radome and 'bent wings' lending the aircraft an almost caricatured appearance. An everyday sight for the hundreds of 'boomers' who spent their time buried in the sterns of countless Stratotankers and Extenders, a Phantom II from this angle could never fail to send a shiver up the spine of a true 'Phanatic'. Wearing the quintessential camouflage scheme for a USAF F-4, an anonymous Delta waits for the fuel to flow, its pilot having driven the 'Rhino' into the appropriate patch of sky for the transfer to take place - if it was not for the 1980s style all-black 'star and bar' on the port wing this photograph could have easily been taken over the jungles of Southeast Asia.

Perfectly illustrating the fashionable 'Europe One' matt scheme that swept through the ranks of the ANG's TAC-gained F-4D units in the mid-1980s, four smoking 'Green Mountain Boys' beat up Burlington International Airport on 3 August 1986, marking the end of the 'Rhino's' residence in Vermont. The closest Phantom II in this 'dirty' formation had previously served with the 48th, 474th and 56th TFWs before arriving at the 134th TFS in January 1982. Along with 65-704, this jet then headed west to the 171st FIS at Selfridge, where the camouflage finish was replaced by gloss ADC gray overall. Initially equipped with P-47Ds when first organized in July 1946, the 134th FS was redesignated an F1S in 1951 and successively equipped with the F-51D, F-94 A/B, F-84D and F-102A/TF-102A.

In June 1974 the 'Green Mountain Boys' swapped their Delta Daggers for the more sedate Martin EB-57, being redesignated the 134th Defense Systems Evaluation Squadron. Despite their long ties to ADC the squadron was transferred to TAC control when it traded in its obsolete EB-57s for F-4Ds in January 1982. The Phantom II's stay in Vermont was comparatively brief, the unit picking up some of the first F-16A/B ADFs delivered to the ANG in July 1987; the 134th became an FIS once again following re-equipment.

Also present at March during the 196th TFS's spell with F-4Cs was 64-0923, the fifth from last Charlie model built for the USAF. A total of 583 F-4Cs were delivered from St Louis before production shifted to the Delta in February 1966. Many of these aircraft flew virtually straight from St Louis to Phan Rang or Cam Ranh Bay, South Vietnam. As the new F-4D (fitted with improved fire-control radar and weapons release computer) became available in larger numbers, the various wings in Southeast Asia rapidly traded up. The war-weary but still essentially low-time Charlies were transferred to units under USAFE, PACAF and CONUS control, replacing F-100s, F-101s and F-105s. Sprayed up in 'Europe One' camouflage almost 20 years after its spell in the combat zone, this ANG warrior was photographed trailing its drag chute moments after touchdown at March on 7 December 1985.

ANG squadrons have developed a strong liking for stars as part of their individual markings over the years, and one of the most spectacular schemes developed was that worn by the 196th TFS, California ANG. Looking arguably too good to fly, this stunning F-4C has certainly reaped the rewards of hours of ANG attention back at March AFB. Like its squadron mates, 63-7553 arrived on the West Coast in decidedly second-hand condition after spending a decade at Luke AFB being abused by 'nugget' pilots assigned to the 58th TTW. Overhauled and resprayed in Southeast Asia camouflage before being declared ready for service, the aircraft underwent a further facelift in September 1984 when it became one of the first F-4s at March to strut its stuff decked out in 'Europe One' colors. Equipped with an AIM-9P on the port rail and an unusually decorative wing tank, this veteran batch one F-4C was photographed cruising off the California coast on 24 October 1984.

(Left & above) March is one of the few bases in today's Air Force that can boast at least one unit from all three organizations that make up the modern USAF. Two-thirds of the 'whole picture' are represented in these impressive photographs of an air refuelling high over the featureless Californian desert. The F-4E is clearly a 196th TFS machine, loaded with four Mk 82 500 lb dummy bombs on the inner pylons, while the glossy KC-135E belongs to the 336th Air Refueling Squadron. Although the 196th TFS were late into F-4s, they more than made up for it by operating three different marks of Phantom II in under a decade. Equipped with F-4Cs between October 1982 and May 1987, the squadron eventually despatched their 'Europe One' Charlies to AMARC and received similarly camouflaged F-4Es in their place. Three years later the elderly Echoes were replaced by decidedly geriatric RF-4Cs, the unit being redesignated the 196th Reconnaissance Squadron. Rumour has it that changes aren't quite over yet for the squadron, the 196th having reputedly been earmarked for re-equipment with KC-135Rs sometime in 1994.

Turning the clock back almost 50 years, the 196th FS (as they were then designated) created Guard history when they became the first squadron to receive jets - a batch of brand new F-80Cs, at Norton AFB in June 1948. Called to arms in October 1950, the squadron flew combat sorties in F-84Es over North Korea until

being returned to state control in July 1952. A spell with F-51Hs followed, before the piston-engined classic was finally retired as surplus ex-Korean War F-86As arrived at Ontario International Airport in March 1954. The unit assumed an air defense role in the mid-1950s as the Alphas were replaced first by Delta and then by Lima models. Its interceptor capability was further improved with the arrival of the Delta Dagger in 1965. In response to the subsequent anti-Vietnam backlash on the West Coast, in 1975 the squadron re-equipped with the diminutive Cessna O-2A forward air control aeroplane instead of the favored F-106 interceptor. After eight years in 'propeller hell' the unit finally returned to its former glory days with the arrival of F-4Cs at their new March facility in 1983.

"I've spotted the Dairy Queen and I'm going in": the lead jet in this three-ship performs an ebullient wheeling break away from his squadron mates. By the time the F-4E became available in sufficient numbers to re-equip ANG Phantom II units a similarly large quantity of early-batch F-16As were also being progressively released from frontline wings as the more potent Charlie model Fighting Falcon came into service. As a result, only five squadrons (four F-4C - 110th, 113th, 163rd and 196th TFSs; and one F-4D - 141st TFS) transitioned onto the penultimate Air Force Phantom II, the Echoes being flown until 1991 when they were replaced by F-16A/Bs (113th and 163rd TFSs), F-15As (110th TFS), KC-135Es (141st TFS) and RF-4Cs (196th TFS).

The middle F-4E in this somewhat unorthodox formation has a practice bomb-adapted triple ejector rack fitted to its starboard pylon, while his wingman totes a blue-striped dummy AIM-9L on his hardpoint. 68-0303 was the first Phantom II to leave St Louis as part of batch F-4E-37-MC which, incidentally, was the largest order of Echo models built by McAir (245 aircraft in total, some of which were later transferred to Israel, Egypt and Turkey). Like many other factory-fresh airframes in this batch, the jet was initially sent to the 479th TFW at Holloman AFB in September 1970. Eight months later the aircraft headed north-west to Nellis AFB and the 57th FWW. During '0303's 14-year association with the wing the aircraft flew all manner of test sorties, trialling new weapons like the General Electric 30mm underwing gun pod, and performing anti-SAM mission training for other frontline crews.

While part of the 57th FWW structure, the jet was usually flown by the 422nd FWS.

With the wing beginning to replace its Phantom IIs with Fighting Falcons, '0303 moved back east to its birthplace at Lambert Field in July 1983, being issued to the then recently re-equipped 110th TFS, Missouri ANG. Usually, once an airframe finds its way into the Guard it stays there; but for some unexplained reason this particular jet (along with several other 110th TFS machines) was sent to the 51st TFW at Taegu AB in South Korea for a temporary spell of duty in 1987 - during its Asian excursion the aircraft was flown by the 497th TFS. It returned to St Louis in late 1988, and was retired to AMARC in May 1991.

(Right) This rare underside view of a 110th TFS F-4E was taken from the WSO's position in a fellow Missouri ANG Phantom II back in June 1989; the Echo's distinctive wing leading-edge slats and chin-mounted M61A1 cannon fairing are both visible. The twin launch rails built specifically for the Sidewinder are fitted to the inboard pylons, while the box fairings at the rear of each hardpoint contain chaff and high intensity flares, programmed to spoof heat-seeking ground-to-air and air-to-air missiles - this modification appeared exclusively on F-4E/Gs, and was designated the AN/ALE-40 system. Another piece of trick kit bolted onto this 'Hill Gray' Phantom II is the AN/AVQ-23A Pave Spike laser designator pod, nestled in the port Sparrow trough.

Seen from alongside the shark-mouthed F-4E from Lambert Field, the Pave Spike becomes more obvious, although the BDU-33-configured triple ejector rack fitted in place of the Sidewinder launcher shows that this is not the jet featured in the underside photograph. Only a handful of Block 36 to 45 F-4Es were wired up to operate the AN/AVQ-23A Pave Spike pod, these being flown by the TAC-assigned 141st (New Jersey ANG), 113th and 163rd TFSs (both Indiana ANG), as well as 'Lindbergh's Own' 110th TFS. The system was essentially an improved version of the USAF's first generation precision avionics vectoring equipment (PAVE), as used with laser-guided ordnance in Vietnam. Capable of daytime operations only, the Pave Spike pod can be used in conjunction with Paveway I and II laser-guided bombs. The garish sharkmouth that featured so prominently on 110th TFS Phantom IIs in the late 1980s only appeared after the unit had traded in their F-4Cs for Echo models in 1985.

64

Some considerable distance from the built-up environs of Lambert Field, an F-4E toting a Maverick missile cruises along the runway to commence an early-morning 'tank busting' sortie over the Echo Whisky 17 range at NAS Fallon, Nevada. Photographed while on a weapons det on 18 July 1987, this jet perfectly illustrates the typical markings worn by a 110th TFS F-4E from 1985 to 1991. The Maverick round wears the blue training bands indicating that it is an inert weapon; however, the 'SCENE MAG' stencilling on its nose confirms that the 'scene magnification' electro-optical (TV) seeker head of the AGM-65B is fully functional. This modification to the standard AGM-65A allows the

WSO to lock up the target from roughly twice the distance.

Currently flying early-build F-15A/Bs at Lambert Field, the 110th FS (as it is now designated) can trace its history back to 23 June 1923 at the very same location, the 110th Observation Squadron being initially equipped with JN-4H Jennys. A succession of biplanes followed up to the outbreak of World War 2, the unit's most famous pilot during this period being Charles Lindbergh. On active duty from December 1940 through February 1946, the squadron flew anti-submarine patrols and worked with the Army prior to being redesignated the 110th Reconnaissance Squadron (Fighter) on 2 April 1943. Assigned to the 71st Reconnaissance

Group, the squadron saw action over New Guinea, the Philippines and Okinawa, equipped successively with the P-39, P-40 and P-51. Upon returning to Lambert Field, and the newly organized Missouri Air National Guard, the unit retained its Mustangs until a further call to active duty in March 1951 saw 'Lindbergh's Own' move to Texas and convert to B-26B/C Invaders, being redesignated the 110th Bombardment Squadron (Light).

Back in St Louis by December of the following year, the unit plugged on with its obsolescent B-26s until spring 1957, when a batch of slightly younger F-80Cs introduced the unit to the jet age in preparation for re-equipment with F-84Fs. Initially assigned to

ADC as the 110ths FIS, the unit transferred to TAC control on 1 January 1960, becoming a TFS in the process. Called to active duty during the Berlin Crisis the following year, the squadron deployed to Toul-Roires in France for almost 12 months of flying with USAFE as part of the temporary 7131st TFW. Upon their return to Lambert Field in August 1962 the unit transitioned onto the F-100 Super Sabre, the 110ths TFS flying the C-, D- and F-models at various times over the next 16 years. F-4Cs finally began to arrive 'back home' in the spring of 1979, thus commencing the squadron's 12-year relationship with the Phantom II.

Many ANG squadrons operated a mix force of 'Europe One' and 'Hill Gray' Phantom IIs towards the end of the 1980s, this lack of uniformity tending to be more prevalent in F-4E units, as the Guardsmen would often receive a steady trickle of ex-frontline airframes still adorned with the older matt scheme. Total resprays were usually handled exclusively by the ALC, and as the time approached for units to transition onto more modern equipment the chore of repainting soon-to-be-retired F-4Es assumed little importance - hence the 50/50 split in this 110th TFS formation, photographed from the boomer's window in a KC-135 high over Missouri in April 1989.

(Right) The ANG's 'universal soldier' for the 1990s leads a diamond formation over the parched plains of Kansas in June 1988. When this impressive photograph was taken the Kansas ANG's 184th TFG was in the process of transitioning its two squadrons from F-4Ds to F-16As - the leader wears the distinctive 'Jayhawk' marking of the newly activated 161st TFTS. The Delta in the diamond belongs to the 127th TFS, which succumbed to F-16A obscurity in 1990. In the trail slot is a visiting A-7D from the 162nd TFS, Ohio ANG, this unit having also recently traded up to the F-16C/D. Finally, the F-4E (which lacks the near-standard dark grey anti-dazzle nose camouflage as worn on the F-4D) was at the time attached to the 163rd TFS at Fort Wayne Municipal Airport, Indiana - like the 162nd TFS, this unit also now flies F-16C/Ds.

McAir's revenge, and not a single Forth Worth fighter in sight. As a last hoorah for the USAF Phantom II, the Kansas ANG's 184th TFG held a 'pharewell' party on 31 March /1 April 1990 to mark the retirement of the type from service with the 127th TFS and 177th TFTS. Invitations were sent out to all remaining Phantom II 'phlyers', and 42 aircraft covering 17 units and four different marks 'phlew' in to McConnell to join the eight remaining 'Jayhawks' F-4Ds. In the line-up closest to the camera from right to left are: an F-4E from the 196th TFS (California ANG); an unmarked 177th TFTS F-4D; two 3246th Test Wing F-4Es from Eglin; a pair of 113th TFS F-4Es (Indiana ANG); two F-4Es from the 4486th Test Squadron at Eglin; a quartet of 110th TFS F-4Es (Missouri ANG); four 141st TFS F-4Es (New Jersey ANG); and a similar number of 704th TFS AFRES F-4Es from Bergstrom AFB (Texas). In the second row from right to left are: a solitary 171st FIS F-4D (Michigan ANG); an RF-4C of the 173rd TRS (Nebraska ANG); another RF-4C, this time from the 153rd TRS (Mississippi ANG); a second 196th TFS F-4E; an F-4D of the 179th FIS Minnesota ANG); three F-4Ds of the 136th FIS (New York ANG); and another unmarked 177th TFTS F-4D. All of these squadrons, bar the 173rd TRS, have now retired their Phantom IIs.

Basking in the mid-August sun at Bergstrom AFB, Texas, during RAM '88, this mixed line-up of RF-4Cs belong to the 106th TRS, Alabama Air Guard ('BH' tailcode) and the recently deactivated 12th TRS 'Blackbirds' of the frontline 67th TRW. Both very experienced operators of the RF-4C, the two squadrons between them had totalled no less than 48 years' flying time on the recce-Phantom II by the beginning of 1993. Although the 106th TRS continue to ply their trade from Sumpter Smith ANGB at Birmingham Municipal Airport, the Bergstrom-based 12th RS was disestablished, along with its parent wing, at its Texas home on 28 August 1992. The three ANG machines heading this line-up all wear unit citations just aft of the starboard lateral camera aperture. With the disbandment of the 12th RS, which had initially formed at Mountain Home AFB, Idaho, on 1 July 1966 as part of the Vietnam build-up, the 106th RS is now the 'senior' RF-4C outfit in the Air Force, having flown them since February 1971.

The squadron was heavily involved in *Desert Shield/Desert Storm* operations in 1990/91, 64-1044 visible in this photograph being one of eleven aircraft sent to the United Arab Emirates. The only casualties of the unit's four-month deployment to the Middle East were suffered when this very aircraft was lost over Abu Dhabi on 8 October 1990 during a low-level training sortie - both Maj.Barry K.Henderson (pilot) and Maj.Stephen G.Schramm (RSO) were killed. The unit's aircraft were despatched to the Gulf primarily because of their Long-Range Oblique Photography (LOROP) suite, the 106th TRS being the only operator of these specially modified RF-4Cs. The modification centres around the KS-127 optical camera, which possesses a focal length of no less than 66 inches; the standard KS-87 camera installed in the aircraft when new was fitted with an 18-inch lens.

(Right) The 106th TRS were sent back to Alabama in December 1990 after completing their operational tour, but the unit's aircraft stayed behind and eventually moved to Sheikh Isa AB in Bahrain on the 19th of that month. By this stage the veteran jets were being flown by crews from the 192nd TRS, Nevada ANG, the 'High Rollers' actually going to war in the RF-4Cs in the new year. As part of the 35th TFW (Provisional) the aircraft were flown on 412 daytime recce sorties, the crews becoming particularly adept at searching out equipment associated with mobile Scud launchers. A further two RF-4Cs (a 192nd TRS jet and a 153rd TRS, Mississippi ANG, machine) were flown out prior to *Desert Storm* as attrition replacements. The unit returned to the US on 8 April 1991, having lost another RF-4C into the Gulf a week prior to leaving the Middle East due to catastrophic engine failure soon after launching from Bahrain; the crew ejected safely.

Photographed in more peaceful skies two and a half years before the conflict, a typically pristine 'High Roller' cruises over the desolate landscape of Nevada. The 192nd TRS was one of two ANG units to transition onto the RF-4C in 1975, the Phantom IIs replacing RF-101Bs at the squadron's Reno-Cannon International Airport facility. Arguably the unofficial 'Topguns' of the ANG recce world, the squadron won the overall competition at two of the three RAMs held between 1986 and 1990. In more recent times the 'High Rollers' almost became a 'Wild Weasel' unit soon after returning from the Gulf. Having received a solitary F-4G from George AFB, the transition was cancelled and the unit's designation changed to the 192nd RS, in line with the Air Force's overall restructuring. The unit is scheduled to replace its RF-4Cs with C-130 Hercules sometime in 1993.

One squadron that recently succumbed to the inevitable was the 153rd TFS, the 'Magnolia Militia', who traded in their RF-4Cs for KC-135Rs. Based at Key Field in Meridian, Mississippi, the unit has a long and distinguished recce pedigree that stretches back to the European Theater in World War 2; and it spent several postwar years equipped with the P-47N and tasked with SAC bomber escort duty. In late 1952 the unit was redesignated a TRS and issued with RF-51Ds, a type it flew until converting to RF-80As in June 1955. Brand new RF-84Fs arrived in Mississippi in 1957 to replace the obsolete Shooting Stars, the 153rd getting over a decade's use out of the rugged Republic Thunderflash before retiring them to Davis-Monthan and receiving RF-101Cs in their place. The last squadron in the USAF to operate the recce-optimized Voodoo, the 'Magnolia Militia' ended a chapter in Air Force history when it finally despatched its last RF-101C to AMARC on 13 January 1979.

Photographed on 4 November 1986, these immaculate RF-4Cs were transitting to Bergstrom AFB for the inaugural RAM. Four years later 66-0425 would find itself in Bahrain, having been sent to Sheikh Isa AB as an attrition replacement for 64-1044. By this stage in the aircraft's long history it had traded in its 'Europe One' camouflage for 'Hill Grays', although the unit's distinctive gold pin-striping had been retained - the 192nd TRS did, however, adorn its fin cap with the traditional 'High Rollers' logo, sprayed on an all-white background.

Just as a morning in the beautician's can restore one's former glory, so too a spell in the ALC can transform a Phantom II from a basket case into the belle of the ball. Photographed cruising over a socked-in Mississippi in November 1988, 65-0935's stained and flaking camouflage contrasts with the satin sheen and shiny tailcone skinning of 66-0423, the former only days away from a trip to Utah and the latter having recently returned. Both these jets had previously served with the 10th TRW at RAF Alconbury in Suffolk in the early 1970s, '0423 having been delivered straight from the St Louis factory to the 30th TRS in May 1967, and '0935 being transferred from the 26th TRW at Zweibrucken, Germany, in June 1975. When the 10th TRW deactivated two of its three squadrons in 1976 both RF-4Cs were allocated to the sole remaining unit, the 1st TRS. With USAFE reducing its recce needs as the decade passed, the two jets were returned to the US in November 1978 and reissued to ANG units, '0935 spending 12 months in the ALC prior to being allocated to the 165th TRS, Kentucky ANG, at Standiford Field, Louisville; '0423 went straight into service with the 153rd TRS. Both aircraft returned to European skies in April/May 1990 as the 153rd TRS deployed to Aviano AB in Italy for exercise *Coronet Saddle*.

(Left) In August 1990 three RF-4Cs from the 173rd TRS (recently redesignated RS) made a brief cross-country flight down to Bergstrom from their Lincoln Municipal Airport facility in Nebraska. The trio had headed south for RAM '90, the competition having started from the moment the aircraft arrived overhead at the Texas base. The unit began the exercise well by finishing second in the Arrival Competition, posting a time just eight seconds over their estimated figure. However, other than a fine second place to the 153rd TFS in the Maintenance Competition, the 173rd failed to make much of an impact in the remaining events. Like many other RF-4C-equipped units, the 173rd TFS has flown several key types of aircraft over the past four decades. It was initially formed in July 1946 and equipped with the ubiquitous P-51D. A brief spell with F-80Cs followed in 1948, the unit becoming one of the first ANG squadrons to convert to jets.

The Shooting Stars were returned to the active duty USAF at the commencement of hostilities in Korea, Mustangs being re-introduced in their place. F-80Cs returned in 1953 and remained with the then 173rd FIS until retired in favor of F-86Ds in January 1957. The ultimate USAF Sabre, the F-86L, was ushered into service with the squadron in late 1959. Four years later the first RF-84Fs arrived, and the unit at last became a TRS. Unlike several other ANG squadrons who flew recce-Voodoos in between operating the Thunderflash and the Phantom II, the Nebraska unit exchanged its Republic aircraft for relatively fresh RF-4Cs in February 1972, thus becoming only the third such user of the 'Rhino' up to that point in the Guard's history. The unit is currently scheduled for conversion to KC-135Rs in 1994/95, although this exchange has not yet been confirmed.

One F-4D retained in the Confederacy was this sparkling example of 'McAir Magic', 66-8788, which originally left St Louis on 24 November 1967. Sent west to the war zone, the aircraft was issued to the famous 8th TFW 'Wolfpack' based at Ubon RTAFB in December 1967. Commanded by the legendary Col.Robin Olds, the wing had gained notoriety in January that year when, during Operation *Bolo*, they downed seven MiGs in a single day. After two years of combat with the 'Wolfpack' the jet exchanged its 'FG' tailcodes for the 366th TFW's 'BT' in late 1969, although it stayed at Ubon. The 'Gunfighters' had also scored heavily during the *Rolling Thunder* years, although '8758 failed to open its account during its spell with the wing. A brief term in South Vietnam with the Phu Cat-based 37th TFW was followed by a spell with the 432nd TRW in 1974/75, again in Thailand; this outfit had claimed

no fewer than 32 MiGs during the *Linebacker* offensive of 1972. Returning to the 8th TFW in late 1975, the aircraft spent the next seven years adorned with the wing's famous 'WP' tailcode at Kunsan AB in South Korea. Following the wing's conversion onto the F-16A in 1982, the F-4D was at last returned to the USA and issued to the recently re-equipped 704th TFS at Bergstrom.

This aircraft initially entered service in Texas still fitted with its distinctive AN/ARN-92 LORAN navigation gear and dorsal 'towel rack' antennas on the spine. Only 71 late-production F-4Ds in blocks 32 and 33, and 20 RF-4Cs, had been modified with this equipment, fitted primarily for long-range strike sorties into North Vietnam. By the time this photograph was taken of a fully armed up '6788 in August 1988 the jet had lost is 'towel rack' and received an updated RWR suite instead. The 704th TFS's unique 'Cloud Scheme' was inspired by the colors worn on the Corsair IIs that equipped several ANG squadrons based in the Midwest.

(Left) The effectiveness of the novel scheme is clearly demonstrated by these two F-4Ds, each is equipped with a pair of travel pods fitted to the inner pylons - the port twin launcher rails on both F-4Ds also appear to be fitted with finless AIM-9 acquisition rounds. Like the Dayton reservists, the 704th TFS's controlling body, the 924th TFG, started life in January 1963 as a C-119 operator. Redesignated a tactical air group in July 1967, the 924th re-equipped with C-130As, which were split between the 704th and 705th Tactical Air Squadrons. The group switched roles in July 1981, its weary C-130Bs being replaced by equally second-hand F-4Ds, which were in turn retired to AMARC seven years later as the first F-4E DMAS (Digital Modular Avionics System) aircraft arrived from the 4th TFW's 336th TFS at Seymour Johnson in North Carolina. Like the four remaining AFRES fighter squadrons, the 704th TFS has now retired its Phantom IIs in favor of the F-16A/B.

Although unable to boast the impressive histories of many of today's ANG units, the relatively new AFRES squadrons are nevertheless equipped with the same aircraft and invariably tasked with similar roles to their state-organized brethren. The major operational difference between the two lies in their structure and role, rather than their hardware and day-to-day mission profiles. The ANG is a state-orientated organization which relies on funding from within its own borders, and in peacetime co-ordinates its activities to best satisfy the people who financially support it. The AFRES, on the other hand, is essentially a part-time 'clone' of the USAF responsible for providing a combat-ready pool of men and machinery to help bolster the ranks of the frontline force in times of emergency. Split into three air forces, the AFRES shares tanker and transport aircraft with full-time units, as well as controlling its own combat types like the F-16, A-10 and AC-130A.

One of five fast jet units within the 10th Air Force is the 89th TFS/906th FG, reformed in line with the Total Force Policy which saw the AFRES assume greater responsibility in the national defense structure. Initially activated in February 1963 as a transport group equipped with C-119 and later C-123K aircraft, the 906th Tactical Cargo Group was eventually stood down during the post-Vietnam cutbacks of 1975. Reformed at Wright-Patterson AFB, Ohio, in July 1982, the group's 89th TFS was issued with 22 refurbished F-4Ds obtained from various frontline and ANG sources. When the aircraft first arrived at the Dayton facility they were camouflaged in Southeast Asia colors, this scheme eventually giving way to matt greys, as worn by these F-4Ds, in 1986. The unit also resprayed the radomes of their jets in a darker shade of grey than was normal for that period. Photographed in September 1989, this immaculate two-ship formation was put up to perform one of the last sorties flown by the 89th TFS prior to its conversion onto the F-16A/B. Both armed with AIM-9Ls, the F-4s have been adorned with stylish nicknames beneath the canopies. The trailing jet came to the 89th TFS from the fellow AFRES-manned 704th TFS based at Bergstrom AFB. Before being issued to the reserves 66-7699 have served with both the 49th TFW at Holloman and 474th TFW at Nellis.

Surrounded by an assortment of ordnance guaranteed to ruin any infantryman's day, a relatively youthful 704th TFS F-4E DMAS awaits the attention of the squadron's armorers on a sunny October afternoon at Bergstrom in 1989. Strapped to the weapons trolley to the right of the 'jammer' are three Mk 76 'blue bombs', while on the left a single CBU-58A cluster bomb unit houses orange-sized anti-personnel bomblets fused to explode on impact. The MJ-1 itself is being driven towards a 'SCENE MAG'

AGM-65B Maverick training round. The bulge on the spine of this jet houses antennae for the Lear-Siegler AN/ARN-101(V) Digital Modular Nav-Attack System, which drastically upgraded the F-4E's ability to get weapons like these smack on target in any weather, 24 hours a day. This particular airframe was among the final batch of 34 Phantom IIs built for the USAF in the early 1970s.

Sharing a similar squadron motif with the 704th TFS is the Carswell-based 457th TFS, who operated the Delta and Echo model F-4s concurrently with their AFRES brethren. Cruising over the flat plains that surround their Texas base on a clear October day in 1989, this brace of F-4Es each carry a pair of dummy Mavericks on the starboard pylons; although inert, each Maverick is equipped with a fully operable acquisition head, the outer missile of each pair being 'SCENE MAG' (AGM-65B) electro-optically guided and the inner devices relying on imaging infra-red (AGM-65D) tracking. The lead F-4E was delivered from the St Louis plant to the 32nd TFS at Soesterburg AB, in the Netherlands, in September 1969. From there it moved to the 86th TFW at Ramstein, Germany, in 1978 following the re-equipment of the 32nd TFS with F-15A/Bs; '0446 finally returned stateside to the 474th TFW at Moody AFB, Georgia, in 1985 when the 86th transitioned onto the F-16C/D. The arrival of Fighting Falcons in

Georgia in January 1988 saw the aircraft heading south for its final USAF posting, its 'MY' tailcodes being swapped for the 'TH' of the 457th TFS/301st TFW.

Unlike most other AFRES wings/groups the 301st TFW has always been in fighters, starting with P-47 Thunderbolts when it was activated at Seymour Johnson in October 1944. Sent to the western Pacific, the wing flew long-range escort for B-29s bombing Japan. Following VJ day the 301st TFW was based in the Okinawan Islands, and re-equipped firstly with the P-61 and then the P-80. Inactivated in January 1949, the wing remained dormant until July 1972 when it was reformed at Carswell AFB, Texas, and issued with war weary F-105Ds. The unit proudly flew these 'Vietnam Vets' until 1981 when they were replaced by F-4Cs.

Close-Up

DANGER

EJECTION SEAT & CANOPY

DANGER

DANGER

Strapped in with the engines rumbling, a reservist from the 704th TFS prepares to take his foot off the brakes, blip the throttle, and roll out to the threshold of the Bergstrom runway. He is attached to the Martin-Baker Mk H7 zero-zero seat by shoulder, lap and crotch harnesses, all of which will tighten immediately after he pulls the D-ring between his legs, or the striped O-rings behind his head, to initiate ejection. Stuffed down the side of the instrument panel shroud are his route maps; the notes on the front of the folded sheets suggest that he will be flying a high altitude cross-country sortie away from Texas for perhaps a few days TDY. The tan-colored material fitted to the front of his HGU-55/P helmet serves a dual purpose - it cuts down the bonedome's reflection within the cockpit transparency, and it stops the helmet from scratching the perspex itself during high G manoeuvring.

After preparing the aircraft mechanically prior to each and every sortie, the 'tecky's' last job before signing the aircraft over to the crew is to give the canopy a thorough polish with a trusty chamois and plenty of 'elbow grease'.

The cockpit switches and dials of this veteran F-4S would be familiar to several generations of Navy and Marine Corps pilots. No CRTs, HOTAS or HUD for the aviators of the Vietnam era: just a dim luminescent scope for the AN/AWG-10A fire control radar, conventional artificial horizon ('Attitude Director Indicator' in McAir-speak) and altimeter gauges, and an optical gunsight atop the cockpit coaming. Although this particular Phantom II would have left St Louis in the late 1960s as an F-4J, the upgrading modification performed by the Naval Aircraft Rework Facility (NARF) a decade later left the cockpit relatively unchanged. As with virtually all American fast jets of the period, the F-4's cockpit gives the casual observer a feeling of sturdiness - just check out that rivet detail holding the side consoles together and the canopy transparency in place...

(Left) Unfortunately, preparing yourself for a Phantom II flight is not like jumping in your car for a quick trip down to the store for a carton of milk. Having stowed your maps and wedged your helmet on the windscreen, the next step is to connect all those tentacle-like harness straps in the proper sequence. An experienced 'phlyer' can slip in and strap on in a matter of moments; for this less seasoned pilot photographed at George AFB in August 1986 the helping hand offered by a line crewman is much appreciated. The tape recorder tucked down beneath the pilot's flight manual will log all voice transmissions made by the crew throughout the flight; this cheap but effective device allows the instructors at the 21st TFTS to debrief the students fully upon their return to George.

Experience is one thing that this AFRES crew does not lack, all pilots and WSOs on the 457th TFS's books having completed at least one frontline tour with a Phantom II-equipped unit prior to joining the reserve. Following a redesign of the original FGH-1's flush canopy by the US Navy prior to the fighter entering large scale production, the USAF's vast Phantom II fleet all shared identical office layouts, with the large transparency area which improved visibility. Towards the end of the aircraft's life with the USAF/ANG some F-4E/Gs had their windscreens replaced by Goodyear Aerospace one-piece transparencies, which offered the pilot better protection against birdstrikes and improved his forward vision. This particular F-4E (68-0449) was originally delivered to the 479th TFW at Holloman AFB in September 1969. From there it passed on to the 347th TFW at Moody AFB before eventually arriving at Carswell in early 1988; it retired to AMARC on 2 April 1991.

(Left) Due to its long USAF service the F-4 featured prominently in many aircrew logbooks, some pilots and WSOs amassing truly phenomenal hour-time figures on the jet. One of those was Lt.Col.Wayne Yarolem, who passed the 5000-hour mark while assigned to the 113th TFS/181st TFG at Hullman Regional Airport in April 1985; his career spanned several variants, and included combat tours in Southeast Asia. Rather appropriately, the jet chosen to honour this occasion was also a combat veteran, 63-7437 having been sent to Thailand in 1966 for the 8th TFW. The 30th F-4C built for the USAF, it served with the 57th FWW at Nellis in the late 1960s, before being returned to Asia and the 18th TFW at Kadena AFB, Okinawa, in 1976. There it performed anti-radar tasks with the 67th TFS 'Supercocks' as an EF-4C 'Wild Weasel IV', this unit having previously flown Shrike anti-radar sorties during the *Linebacker* offensive in December 1972 from Korat RTAFB. After a long spell within PACAF the aircraft returned to the USA following the 18th TFW's re-equipment with F-15s. At about the same time the 113th TFS was transitioning from F-100Ds to F-4Cs, and this aircraft was immediately assigned to the ANG squadron. There, its 'Wild Weasel' capabilities were deleted and it flew purely as a conventional TAC fighter/bomber. Like Lt.Col. Yarolem, 63-7437 retired from the ANG in late 1987.

Nose gear door art: capable of making even more noise than Mick Jagger and The Rolling Stones, 'Lips III' was the nickname given to a 110th TFS F-4E.

May 1989: F-4C 65-0692 of the 136th FIS, New York ANG, displays the controversial MIA symbol on its door, both the badge and the ' Iron Butterfly' nickname being applied as decals.

The 'eyes' of the F-4C, the bulky AN/APQ-100 fire control radar: by the time this excellent detail shot was taken in April 1990 the system had long since been removed from the Top Secret list. The later Westinghouse AN/APQ-120 system fitted into the F-4E benefitted from solid-state avionics and an overall reduction in size of both the radar equipment itself and the tracking scanner. The large 32-inch dish of the original AN/APQ-100 forced McAir technicians to design the distinctive bulbous radome that was to become such a feature of the early model Phantom IIs.

(Right, above) The distinctive square panel fitted flush to the former cannon fairing on the F-4G covers four large and five small spiral helix antennas, which receive radar signals in the mid/high bands. This dedicated 'missile-buster' carries no fewer than 52 separate antennas and aerials on its fuselage.

(Right, below) Late-build F-4Es embodied a number of improvements over their older brothers including bigger leading-edge slats, a lengthened cannon fairing and, perhaps most obvious of all, this cylindrical fairing on the port wing housing the TISEO (Target Identification System, Electro-Optical). Developed by Northrop in response to USAF experience in Southeast Asia with both guided and unguided weapons, the TISEO consisted of a powerful TV camera fitted with a 1200 mm zoom lens. The images collected by the camera were relayed in real time to a screen positioned near the WSO's radar display - the system was restricted to fair weather operability only. The forward section of the housing contained the lens and the converter assembly, while the rear portion closest to the wing protected the Stabilization Generator equipment.

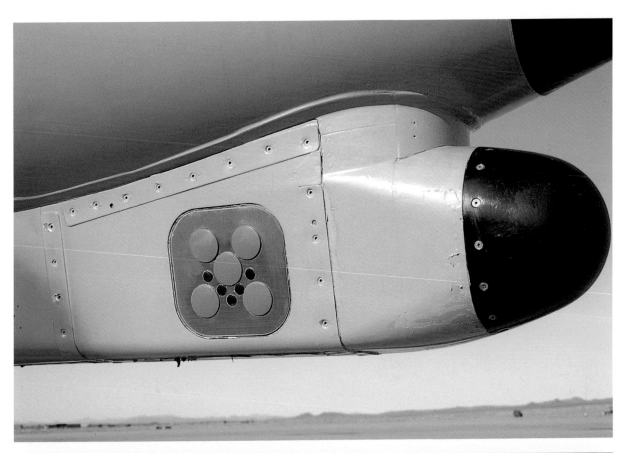

As an aircraft progresses through its service life the once clean and unencumbered airframe that countless aerodynamicists and designers spent months creating is festooned with various permanent and bolt-on excrescences which service experience has shown will help the crew stay alive in combat. The Tracor AN/ALE-40 chaff/flare dispenser appeared on the F-4E late in its career. Up to eight of these boxes could quickly be scabbed onto the aircraft's weapons pylons, the system being manually fired by the pilot or WSO. Each device contained 30 tubes which could be filled with either chaff bundles or high intensity flares; both had to be fired aft. This particular dispenser is fully loaded, but yet to be rendered 'live' - the safety pin and associated dayglo tag are still in place.

A FOD's (foreign object debris) eye view of the port intake ducting of a 465th TFS F-4D; note the chalked 'SH' lettering on the engine intake compressor face.